Third Cord Secret

Third Cord Secret

Discover the Secret of a Highly Successful Marriage

Alan & Jamie Wood

Mobile Alabama

Third Cord Secret—Discover the Secret of a Highly Successful Marriage
by Alan & Jamie Wood

ISBN 978-1-58169-316-4
For Worldwide Distribution
Printed in the U.S.A.

Gazelle Press
P.O. Box 191540 • Mobile, AL 36619
800-367-8203

Dedication

We would like to dedicate this book
to our parents—Harriet and Jim
and Joyce and Tom.

We gratefully express our gratitude
to them for raising us in a stable, loving,
Christian home and by particularly
modeling an Ecclesiastes 4:12
marriage.

Table of Contents

Foreword

(Alan) When Jamie and I had been married just over two years, we found ourselves in grave danger. We were both Christians, but we had failed to achieve the spiritual intimacy spoken of in Scripture as "two becoming one."

We searched for the answers to our question, "How can we be led by God in our marriage?" We knew that God wanted our marriage to succeed. Now it was at *this* place that God had us right where He wanted us—ready to ask for *His* help. We cried out, "God, show us how to live in harmony as one. You know what we need to know. You know what needs to happen. Please show us. Help!" Perhaps you too have found yourself in this place.

Convinced that God had already provided us with every tool, we sought the secret. Once revealed, that secret would make a difference—a difference that would lead us into a highly successful marriage. Now, twenty-four years into our marriage, we enjoy the exhilarating, empowering transformation of this most important secret.

What is the secret? God cares about the details of our lives so much so that He sent us the Helper! Jesus said, *"The Helper, the Holy Spirit, the Spirit of truth, whom the Father will send, in my name, will teach you all things and remind you of the things that I have told you"* (John 14:26). He *is* the Third Cord that binds a marriage together. The Holy Spirit is ready to help your marriage succeed.

Chapter One

Come Holy Spirit

(Jamie) We were struggling in our marriage. Some twenty years ago, almost three years into our marriage, we had reached a point where we didn't like each other very much. It appeared to those around us that we had the world by the tail; on the outside, everything looked great. But in reality, we weren't doing so well. We were just going through the motions. What was missing from our relationship was intimacy. Our conversations had no depth but were just surface talk, a transferring of information. We didn't understand what had happened to our relationship or know how to repair it.

An undercurrent of anger hindered communication; our love was immature and selfish. I had expressed many times a need for change. However, one night, we experienced an "ah-ha" moment. We both sat on the edge of the bed. After being unable to bear another day with an angry man, I said, "We might need to consider divorce." Up to this point, neither of us had ever used that word in the context of our own marriage. As we looked at one another, Alan began to cry. It was then that I realized that this was not what he wanted either. I began to cry. I was relieved to know that he'd decided he was in it for the long haul. Now we were on to something—but what?

Our life together was a mess. We were not satisfied with the way things were. We were ready to ask God for guidance. Because of our willingness, the Holy Spirit was ready to rescue us from ourselves. We had given Him permission to reveal those things we needed to know in order to communicate better with one another.

> *And I* [Jesus] *will ask the Father, and He will give you another Comforter (Counselor, Helper, Intercessor, Advocate, Strengthener and Standby) that He may remain with you forever—The Spirit of Truth, Whom the world cannot receive (welcome, take to its heart), because it does not see Him, for He lives with you and will be in you* (John 14:16-17 AMP).

The Holy Spirit plays a supporting role in His relationship with us. The Greek word *parakletos*, translated as "helper" literally means, "one who is called beside (by our side)." He is the fulfillment of Jesus' promise to never leave us nor forsake us. In order to activate the power of the Holy Spirit, we must first acknowledge Him. Then we must ask Him into our lives, giving Him permission to change things, leaving the old unprofitable things behind.

> *If you . . . know how to give good gifts [gifts that are to their advantage] to your children, how much more will your heavenly Father give the Holy Spirit to those who ask and continue to ask Him!* (Luke 11:13 AMP).

God wants to help us by offering us "a good gift": the assistance of the Holy Spirit as the Helper, "the one who is called beside." *He will* transform every aspect of our lives. *"So I say, live by the spirit; and you will not gratify the desires of your sinful nature"* (Galatians 5:16 NIV).

In our spiritual lives together, as husband and wife, inviting the Holy Spirit welcomes His divine power into our marriage. This is of vital importance because the Holy Spirit is every inch a gentleman. He waits for an invitation to come into relationship with us. He never barges into our lives when He is not wanted. The Holy Spirit desires to be a trusted friend and counselor to us and wants to be approached by us as a beloved grandfather from whom we receive sound advice.

You may wonder, "How will I know when the Holy Spirit is speaking to me?" Great question and the answer is key to understanding every thing else we have written. The Holy Spirit is the manifestation of Jesus' promise to never leave nor forsake us. The fulfillment of that promise is the Holy Spirit. In John 14:27, Jesus says, "Peace I leave with you; my own peace I now give and bequeath to you. Not as the world gives do I give to you. Do not let your heart be troubled neither lem them be afraid."

The primary way in which you will know that you have heard from the Holy Spirit is a manifestation of peace. You will have the peace from God that surpasses all understanding (Philippians 4:7). Your circumstances may be difficult and chaotic, but within your spirit, when you have heard from God, there is perfect peace.

"A cord of three strands is not quickly torn apart" is from a Scripture verse in Ecclesiastes 4:12 (NASU) that so perfectly depicts the relationship of the husband, the wife, and the Holy Spirit. If you have ever seen a rope that has been cut in half, you can see how the three pieces wrap neatly and are fitted around each other for strength.

However, they also can be separated into three individual strands. As all three of these pieces are fitted within the grooves and brought together, they form a thick, strong rope that is difficult to break apart. We need to have a similar picture in our minds of the husband, wife, and Holy Spirit relationship. The Holy Spirit as the third cord facilitates the transformational journey to oneness described in Scripture.

We need never fear the leading of the Holy Spirit because He always leads in accordance with God's will. According to Romans 8:27 AMP, the Holy Spirit *"**intercedes** and pleads [before God] in behalf of the saints according to and in harmony with God's will"* (emphasis added). According to John 16:8, the Holy Spirit reveals truth concerning sin. First Corinthians 12:4-11 reveals that the Holy Spirit bestows divine gifts. If we ask God before we act, He *will* lead us in our interactions with our spouse.

> *(Alan)* Jamie and I led a couple's small group on inviting the Holy Spirit into their marriages. One of the guys in our group had been separated from his wife and young daughters. He always came alone even though we had also invited his wife. She was tired of giving him chance after chance to work on their marriage without seeing results. But he was faithful to participate.
>
> Since this young man had come from a broken home, he didn't have a father in the house to teach him how to be a father or husband. Each week, as we would meet together, we would teach him biblical concepts regarding his role as husband and father. When praying over him, we would ask the Holy Spirit to show him how to be the man that God desired for him to be.
>
> With time he began to change, and his wife took note. As she did, her heart began to soften towards him. Their relationship as husband and wife was being restored. They were communicating again, regaining trust and love for one another. The Holy Spirit was an ***advocate*** for their

marriage, releasing the spirit of reconciliation into their hearts and bonding them together again as one. *"Now all things are of God, who has reconciled us to Himself through Jesus Christ, and has given us the ministry of reconciliation"* (2 Corinthians 5:18 NKJV).

Several months later, we received a letter from his wife. The following is an excerpt from that letter:

Dear Jamie and Alan,
Words simply cannot express our gratitude! Your ministry has truly touched our family. Our marriage has been transformed!

Not only was the Holy Spirit the husband's advocate throughout this time, but He was also was a ***standby*** and ***counselor*** as this young man was learning how to relate to his wife. The Holy Spirit came alongside him and instructed him. We sat back and watched the Holy Spirit work wonders in recreating their marriage!

We recently watched a movie called *Evelyn*, which is a beautiful story of how the Holy Spirit is supposed to work. It is a true account of an Irish man, Desmond Doyle, whose wife abandons the family, leaving him with three children to rear alone. At the time, he had no steady work so his children were taken away from him by the state. He wants to fight for custody but is told that any efforts would be futile. He decides, however, to take his case to court. There is a scene in the courtroom where Desmond is on the stand being questioned.

The judge says, "The fundamental building block of society is the holy family. How can you raise your children without a mother?"

Desmond replies, "The building block in society is not the holy family, but the Holy Trinity—the Father, the Son, and the Holy Spirit. When my mother died, Dad brought us up with the Holy Spirit to guide him. The Bible says faith, hope, and love; but the greatest of these is love. I've given up the drink. I've worked all of the hours God sends. I've become a better person to try and fill myself with the Holy Spirit so I can bring my kids up surrounded by love. That is all I can do. No man can do more."

The story has an even more powerful ending. Not only does Desmond win custody of his children, but because of his valiant fight, many other children from orphanages are also reunited with their families. This one court decision would impact the lives of hundreds in a monumental way.

As Desmond discovered, the key to understanding God's wisdom lies within the Spirit of God. No individual possesses the ability to know God or God's wisdom. The Spirit knows the things of God because the Holy Spirit is the expressed Spirit of God. The Spirit therefore is the link between God and man that makes knowing God possible.

God uses the Holy Spirit to reveal wisdom to us. All we need to do is ask Him to come into relationship with us. He will be a helper, a counselor, an advocate, an intercessor, a strengthener, and a comforter to us if we will only ask. He wants a relationship with us. What a thought: the Creator of the universe, God, the Holy Spirit, wants a relationship with us!

The marriage relationship can be an ever growing revelatory experience in knowing our spouse and God. It is God's intent to have us live a more enriched life through the marriage union. Life will be better and stronger through the power of the Holy Spirit working in our lives. Over the years, we've benefited immensely from an intimate relationship with the Holy Spirit and His transforming power.

Be eager and strive earnestly to guard and keep the harmony and oneness of [and produced by] the Spirit in the binding power of peace. [There is] one body and one Spirit—just as there is also one hope [that belongs] to the calling you received—[There is] one Lord, one faith, one baptism, One God and Father of [us] all, Who is above all [Sovereign over all], pervading all and [living] in [us] all (Ephesians 4:3-6 AMP).

A PRAYER FOR YOUR MARRIAGE

Dear Lord,
Thank You for the Holy Spirit, the Third Cord that binds us together as one. We invite the person of the Holy Spirit to come alongside us to help us be the best that we can be. I thank You that by this invitation we will see the power of God manifested on behalf of our marriage. Thank You for Your promise to never leave us or forsake us. It is our desire to "be eager and strive earnestly to guard and keep harmony and oneness of [and produced by] the Spirit in the binding power of peace" (Ephesians 4:3 AMP).

Chapter Two

Adam's Rib

(Alan) My experience has confirmed the picture our Creator painted for us. My wife, Jamie, is my counterpart, my completer! The things that I am not, she is. Our spirits are blended together as one so much so that on many occasions we have identical thoughts and prayers. We will quite often complete each other's sentences. During the gas shortage caused by Hurricane Katrina's devastation of the Gulf Coast, Jamie made a decision to fill her car with gas only once a week. The thirty dollars that normally filled the car tank now would only buy three quarters of a tank. She prayed that God would extend the gas so that she could drive for the entire week on one tank. She also asked God to help her to be a better planner and steward of her car trips. That evening at home Jamie asked me to agree with her in prayer that this could be accomplished. Unknown to her, I had already prayed the identical prayer that day, asking God to do the same for me. I had also decided to spend only thirty dollars for gas.

Be careful if you make a woman cry, because God counts her tears. The woman came out of a man's rib—not his feet to be walked on, not his head to be superior, but from the side to be equal. She came from under the arm to be protected and next to the heart to be loved (Matthew Henry).

From the very beginning, God intended men and women to complete each other through marriage. Genesis 2:7 (AMP) says, *"God formed man from the dust of the ground and breathed into his nostrils the breath or the spirit of life into him and man became a living being."* How wonderful it is to know that our Creator formed us and then gave us the spirit of life. Our spirits within us cry out for relationship with our Father as our Creator. Adam experienced a direct and intimate fellowship unlike any since the fall of man with his Daddy, God.

Have you ever wondered why God created us in the way that He did from the dust of the earth? Why didn't He create us as He did all the other animals? His creation of us was radically different! God created the animals according to their kind or species. They have a physical body and a soul consisting of their mind, will, and emotions.

Sometimes while walking our 100 pound male golden retriever, he will set his mind to go somewhere that I don't want him to go. His will and emotions combine with his body, and he is hard to handle. He lacks one thing that we humans have—a spirit! We were created in the likeness and image of God.

But what does that mean? God doesn't have a physical body because He is Spirit, right? I'm speaking of our spirit man, which was created in the image of God. Since God is a Spirit, our spirits were created to resemble His. God created us and designed us uniquely for relationship and intimacy with Him. The God of the universe, the Creator of all things, our Father, put a spirit within us that resembles Him. Amazing but true, His heart's desire is for an intimate relationship with us because He loves us deeply!

We were designed with a spirit, a soul, and a physical body. In order for us to have that intimate relationship with God, our spirits must come alive and be filled with His Spirit. That is what happens when we invite Him into our lives. We get what Scripture calls a down payment of the Holy Spirit into our spirits. When this happens, we become alive to Him, and we can begin to enjoy intimacy with Him.

In the beginning, God made Adam in His image. How interesting that when Adam was formed, he held within him, woman, Eve. Adam is a name used for the first man and is a generic noun identifying "man" and "woman" collectively and revealing their origin. First Corinthians 11:8-9 (NAS) says, *"For man does not originate from woman, but woman from man; for indeed man was not created for the woman's sake, but woman for man's sake."*

God noticed that Adam had no one on earth to relate to and no one suitable or compatible with him, and this was *not good*. So He caused Adam to fall into a deep sleep. God took one of his ribs from Adam and formed it into the woman, Eve. However, the Hebrew word that is translated as "rib" in the King James Version of the Bible is *tselaé,* meaning, "side or rib or beam." In the King James Bible, tselaé is translated as "side" in nineteen of the forty-one times it is used. It is only translated twice as "rib."

This gives an entirely new meaning to what God actually did with Adam. God caused Adam to fall asleep, and then He took a side from Adam, closed up the flesh, and used the female side of Adam to form Eve. There is symmetry in the creation as God took Adam's side and fashioned a complementary half or counterpart for Adam. When God presented Eve to him, Adam's response was, "Wo-man, this is my flesh and my bone!"

How often have you heard a man comment that his wife is his "better half"? This phrase refers to the biblical account of creation. God created the perfect companion (completer) for Adam. You've heard a man say of his spouse, "She made my life complete," or "She is my complement." Just as a complementary angle has a common side shared by another angle, so also did Adam and Eve share the same side to complete each other. We become a better *one* through marriage.

> *(Alan)* We have a common side, yet different skills and abilities. Jamie is a gifted artist, painting beautiful images of people and places in pastels and oils. I am not able to draw stick people. On the other hand, I am an accountant; numbers are constantly flying around in my head. I pay the bills, balance the checkbook, and manage our family finances. When I talk numbers and finances, Jamie's eyes glaze over.

So where are we now that God did this wonderful thing in creating us both male and female? God certainly intended that we complete each other through marriage, but how? Scripture says that a man is to leave his father and mother and cleave to his wife. The two shall become one flesh. God's command is to become one again, as we were created in oneness through Adam.

The man is to leave his parents and cleave unto his wife. In other words, the husband is to cling to, stick to, adhere to, and be joined to, his wife inseparably. The marriage between a husband and wife is a bonding of two bodies into one. For example, epoxy glue is formed when two separate entities are blended together to form one strong, permanent bond. A couple has two individual parts that when joined together function better. Ecclesiastes 4:9-10 (NAS) says,

> *Two are better than one because they have a good return for their labor. For if either of them falls, one will lift up his companion. But woe to the one who falls and there is not another to lift him up.*

(Alan) We had just arrived home from a family vacation to

New York City. Returning home on Christmas Eve, I was coming down the spiral staircase in our home, carrying an empty suitcase. Stepping on the narrow part of the stairs with the suitcase in front of me, I lost my footing and fell knee first onto the tile floor in our downstairs den. I tried to get up but immediately fell down again. I quickly realized something was very wrong. As we met with a doctor in the emergency room, we were told that I had severed my quadricep muscle from my kneecap. That is why I had been unable to walk on that leg. Needless to say, if Jamie and my son, James, had not been there to pick me up and carry me to the car, I would have been unable to walk. So I understand the meaning quite literally, If one falls and there is not another to lift him up . . . woe to the one who falls (Ecclesiastes 4:10).

Husbands and wives are intended to be counterparts to each other to bring different strengths, abilities, and virtues into the marriage relationship. The purpose of God to create a helpmate conveys the essence of a counterpart. It is a person who completes another. The word *helpmate* does not suggest weakness or subservience of one spouse to the other, but conveys the concept that "together we're better." The John and Stasi Eldredge books, *Wild at Heart* and *Captivating*, are wonderful tools to help a spouse better understand his or her counterpart.

(Alan) Jamie and I fit together like puzzle pieces. Our differences complement each other, and we are stronger because of those differences. We make a great team! If you don't feel that you fit like puzzle pieces with your spouse, we have great news. The Holy Spirit can help recreate you so that you do fit!

> Jamie is very discerning as it relates to people and motives for behavior. In business situations, she can easily identify people who have inner motives contrary to their outward appearance. Most women have a greater ability to discern situations than men do. Husbands would do well to encourage and listen to their spouse's discernment regarding business partners or in matters concerning relationships.

We have a friend whose husband designed a product. The product could be used in his industry but would not qualify as a conflict of interest with his businesses products. However, to be on the safe side, he went to his sales manager and asked if it would be all right to market the product on his own. His manager told him it was fine.

When he shared this conversation with his wife, she suggested that he also get his manager's permission in writing. He disagreed, saying his manager was a man of his word. Later, the president of his company got wind of this business venture. When the company president came to my friend's husband, he explained that his sales manager had given him permission to do so. His sales manager denied knowing anything about it. Our friend's husband was fired from his job because he had no proof of the agreement. Husbands, listen to your wife's input. If the husband had listened, he could have saved his job.

God created man in His image for relationship and spiritual intimacy with Him. God saw that it was not good for Adam to be alone, so He pulled from Adam his female side to fashion Eve. He designed a counterpart perfect for him!

In the garden when Adam and Eve chose to walk away from God, they lost the intimate relationship they had with the Holy Spirit. At that moment, everything changed. They were no longer in harmony but began a cover up—both literally and figuratively. Adam blamed Eve, and Eve blamed the serpent for their disobedience to God. Their choice brought separation and fault finding into their relationship.

Jesus' sacrifice for us was intended to restore our relationship with God. This restoration of relationship with God reinstates our access to the Holy Spirit, which enables us to pursue restoration of relationship with others. God's plan for marriage is for the husband and wife to complete each other by becoming one again so we can benefit from each other's strengths, abilities, and virtues. The Holy Spirit is the Third Cord that binds us together. God's creation is wonderful to behold! We can experience the beauty of His creation, in the fullness of completion, as we become one again through marriage.

A PRAYER FOR YOUR MARRIAGE

Dear Lord,
Thank You that we complete each other through marriage. You made us so that the spirit within us cries out for relationship with You. We need You, Lord. Help us to be bound together as one through the power of the Holy Spirit and to benefit from each other's strengths, abilities, and virtues. Help us to be perfect counterparts. We agree with Your Word that says, "Two are better than one, because they have a good [more satisfying] reward for their labor" (Ecclesiastes 4:9 AMP).

Chapter Three

Forever Yours

(Jamie) As a young girl, I remember asking my mother, "What is most important about marriage?" She told me that commitment was most important. If you believed in commitment, marriage would last. She said that if everyone understood the seriousness of the marriage covenant, divorce would not be so common.

My mother would later be diagnosed with a crippling disease known as Multiple Sclerosis (MS). She was affected by it slowly. First her steps became unsteady, later she needed to use a cane, and then a walker was necessary. Eventually she was in a wheelchair until she became bedridden. My father took such good care of her over the years. He even retired early because he wanted to be the one to care for her. When he came home after being out in public, he immediately washed his hands before doing anything else to protect her from any possible infection.

He did everything for her, especially in the later years when she had no use of her limbs. They had a mutual appreciation and respect for each other until the end of her life. Many husbands, whose wives have MS, divorce because the men are unable to handle the physical and emotional challenges of caring for their wives with this illness. I will be forever grateful to my parents for the love and commitment they shared and modeled for us, their children.

In his book, *A Promise Kept*, Dr. Robertson McQuilkin relates his decision to attend to his wife, Muriel, an Alzheimer's victim, rather than continue his presidency of Columbia International University. "The decision was made, in a way, forty-two years ago when I promised to care for Muriel 'in sickness and in health . . . till death do us part. I love Muriel. She is a delight to me . . . I don't *have* to care for her. I *get* to! It is a high honor to care for so wonderful a person."

> *For the Lord, the God of Israel says: "I hate divorce and marital separation and him who covers his garment [his wife] with violence. Therefore keep a watch upon your spirit, that you deal not treacherously and faithlessly [with your marriage mate]"* (Malachi 2:16 AMP).

Notice this Scripture specifically addresses "keeping a watch on your spirit" in the context of the marriage relationship. If our spirits are engaged with the Holy Spirit, meaning that we give the Holy Spirit permission to change things, then the Holy Spirit can help navigate us through the troubled waters in marriage. And since we already know that the Holy Spirit only leads in accordance with God's will, we need not worry.

We know a couple who came to us for counsel. Prior to their marriage, they met on campus as college students and promptly became sexually active. Their marriage had been a struggle because she had dealt with mental and emotional instability for years. She had suffered with depression and frequently would leave their home without giving her husband any idea of where she had gone. They didn't know how to communicate with each other. They wondered if it was time to get a divorce.

Becoming Christians shortly after their marriage, they knew enough to seek out Scripture on the subject of divorce. To their great disappointment, they realized it was not biblically acceptable. That is when they got busy. They became serious about making their marriage work. They committed to stay together, inviting the Holy Spirit into their relationship. They began to pray together and for each other. As the Holy Spirit revealed truth to them, they were careful to follow His instruction.

Over time, they were able to deal with each issue victoriously. It was not always easy, but it was well worth the effort. Today they are still together and have two beautiful children who give them even more reason to work hard at their relationship. It all started because of their decision to commit themselves to one another in marriage. This couple kept a watch over their spirits, and God blessed them.

Divorce was a problem in Israel too. Throughout the ancient Near East, all marriages were legally binding contracts. Only Israel upheld marriage as a spiritual covenant worthy of a lifelong commitment. Although divorce had been allowed by law, God expressly rejected the breaking of marital vows in any way. *"The Pharisees said, 'Moses permitted a man to write a certificate of divorce, and to dismiss her.' Jesus replied, 'Moses did that in recognition of your hardness of heart but it was not what God had originally intended'"* (Matthew 19:8). Ultimately, the answer to this controversial issue does not lie in legal, traditional, or human practice but in God's own creative design. God never accommodates or compromises His principles but redeems and restores anyone who seeks His forgiveness.

Today, many couples see divorce as a viable option to an unhappy marriage. "If it doesn't work out, we can always get a divorce." This selfish way of thinking is so prevalent in our society that no one thinks twice about it; the same is true for Christians, who supposedly have a higher standard. Our society resists commitment because it implies "long term."

We are impatient people who readily excuse unpleasant experiences as so-called mistakes. The following statements are common excuses:

- "If I don't like it, I don't have to tough it out. It's too much effort."
- "It is the other person's fault anyway—not mine."
- "I just made a mistake and picked the wrong person."
- "I've fallen out of love. It happens. When I find that right person, *then* I can make a go of it."

All of these defensive words are self-centered. Why do you think there are so many people living together or randomly sleeping together? Society condones it, but these behaviors are about being self-satisfied and wanting instant gratification due to lack of patience and self-control. Among the fruits of the Spirit are patience, self-control, and peace. Galatians 5:5 (AMP) says, *"For we through the Spirit's help, by faith, anticipate and wait for the blessing and good for which our righteousness and right standing with God bring hope."*

(Jamie) We have a friend whose son was in an unhappy marriage. The son and his wife had young children. When the son began speaking of divorce to his father, his father said, "If you think you are unhappy now, just wait until there is another man raising your children. You won't see your kids on holidays, and squabbling with your ex will be even worse because you will be fighting over the children." The son decided it was best to work through his marital

problems. It was good advice from Dad. Realizing the consequences and the inconvenience of divorce motivated the son to work out his problems with his wife. I am reminded of the saying that I saw posted in a school office: "Real love demands you do what's best for your children and not always what's easiest for you."

There are many different reasons why couples are not faithful; however, lack of commitment is the bottom line. How do we remain faithful? We need to know that *"God leads with unfailing love and faithfulness all those who keep His covenant and obey His decrees"* (Psalms 25:10 NLT). Call on the Spirit to give you wisdom in working through issues with your spouse. God is faithful to honor obedience. He just has to have something with which to work. The Holy Spirit is always available for us; all we need do is ask for His help!

Gary Smalley has a book called *Love Is a Decision*. In it, he explains a principle of responding to your spouse. The motivation should not be because of your love for them because there are going to be times when you don't feel very loving towards them. No, your response should come out of the fullness of love for Christ. And with that mindset comes an attitude change toward your spouse, because now it is not based on their behavior but is instead a supernatural, unconditional love.

Dr. McQuilkin made the decision to unconditionally love and care for his wife, Muriel, based upon his vows before God and the marriage witnesses forty-two years earlier on their wedding day. After twenty-two years as president of Columbia International, Dr. McQuilkin resigned his position in order to care for Muriel full time. "The decision to come to Columbia was the most difficult I have had to make; the decision to leave twenty-two years later, though painful, was one of the easiest."

Our commitment to the marriage relationship is very important. We need not worry if in the past we have not had a strong commitment to our marriage. If we make the commitment now, and God will forgive and forget about the past as well as help us to forget about it also. Through the power of the Holy Spirit, He is able to heal relationships so that when problems arise, the decision is not about cutting and running but about the steps that need to be taken to fix it. By inviting the Holy Spirit as the Third Cord into our marriage, we experience revelation power for a divine result.

A PRAYER FOR YOUR MARRIAGE

Dear Lord,
I pray that we will never again take our commitment to one another lightly. I pray we would be God-fearing. Help us to avoid selfishness and consider others before ourselves; and as we are more Spirit-led, we will operate in the fruits of the Spirit with patience, self-control, and peace in our relationship. Thank You for sending the Helper, the One who comes alongside us to guide and instruct us. Most importantly, I pray that we would aid in breaking the cycle of divorce in our society and that through love we serve one another (Galatians 5:13).

Chapter Four

God's Gifts

(Alan) For years I have asked to know God's ways. I often hear from God when I run outside. One day while running, I saw a picture of a banquet table in my mind's eye. In a large room, there sat Jesus seated at the far end. The table was massive surrounded by many high back chairs. It was set with golden goblets, crystal, silver, and beautiful candelabras. On the table, there was every kind of sumptuous food imaginable: meats, fruits and vegetables, beautiful desserts—the epitome of a Thanksgiving feast. Nine-foot tall angels stood at the large, opened wooden doors.

But as the individuals came into the room, no one would sit at the table. Instead, people were coming in and reclining on the floor of the room with their own brown bag lunches. Out of the bags came stale, moldy sandwiches, brown bananas, rotten apples, and food that appeared inedible. Yet, they were eating these lunches. I remember asking God, "Why is no one sitting at the table? And why are they eating *this* food when they could be eating *that* food?"

Jesus had a tear in his eye because no one was feasting on what God had prepared. I understood that the feast represented God's gifts for us as His children. Who would choose to eat rotten food on the floor when a feast at the Lord's magnificent table waits? But this is what we often do when we refuse to ask for or receive God's gifts. We do it our way without considering God's leading. Little by little, the individuals on the floor began to notice the delicacies at the table and moved to the table to partake of it.

Story shared by a Bible teacher: "Jesus was escorting a person on a visit to heaven. They came to a large room with beautifully wrapped boxes of all shapes, sizes, and colors. The boxes reached high and as deep as the eye could see. When asking Jesus what these presents were, He explained, they were the unopened gifts God's children had never asked for and therefore never received"

If you . . . know how to give good gifts to your children, how much more shall your heavenly Father give the Holy Spirit to those who ***ask*** *him* (Luke 11:13 NAS, emphasis added).

Why are there so many unopened gifts in heaven? It is because so many feel unworthy of God's best. From where do those thoughts of unworthiness originate? From Satan? Has someone made us feel that a gift from God cannot be received until we earn or deserve it? How well do we understand the character of God?

Does any one person *ever* deserve God's gifts, even in a lifetime? No. So what are we waiting for? Grace is available for us every day, especially when we fall short. Our God is *full* of grace. Some people have the impression that God is stern and harsh, but that is not true. The Bible says, *"The Lord is gracious and compassionate, slow to anger and rich in love"* (Psalms 145:8 NIV).

Why do we have so many questions about God's character? Because how we see God and how we relate to Him is foundational in having a spirit to Spirit relationship with Him. It is a matter of trust. It is impossible to have a solid relationship with anyone, much less true intimacy, unless we can trust that individual.

David, who eventually became King David, *did* understand and trust God and His character. King David was a great leader who made some big mistakes. He plotted and killed a man, Uriah, in order to hide the fact that he'd had an affair and impregnated Uriah's wife, Bathsheba. After the prophet, Nathan, addressed the sin, David immediately confessed and repented.

The moment David saw that his sin had come between him and God, he immediately asked for forgiveness. He was more concerned about not being in fellowship with God than anything else. Think of all the many hours David had spent with God, writing psalms and praising Him while shepherding. He was developing intimacy with God and meditating on His goodness. Psalms 23:6 (The Message) (written by David) says, "[God's] *beauty and love chase after me every day of my life.*"

David had complete understanding that nothing could separate him from the love of the Father *except* his own sin. Isaiah says, "*But your iniquities have separated you from your God; And your sins have hidden His face from you, so that He will not hear*" (Isaiah 59:2 NKJ). David did not allow a guilty conscience (Satan's condemnation) to separate him from his Father. He had a keen knowledge of God's grace and was fully able to receive God's gift of unconditional love. As soon as he had taken the matter to the Lord with a repentant heart, he *knew* that he was indeed forgiven by Almighty God. It was forgotten. Once relationship was restored, he could resume his position with God.

The Bible describes David as "a man after God's own heart." God longs for us just as He did for David. He desires for us to have an inside "heart change." Intimacy with the Father keeps the heart soft toward Him. His kindness is meant to bring us to repentance.

David trusted God. He trusted that God knew best. Like David, we must truly trust Him in order to invite Him into our marriages. God wants our marriages to be the best they can be. Sending the Holy Spirit was God's gift to empower us to do just that. We know that the Bible is God's instruction manual for life, but without the power of the Holy Spirit to reveal our true condition, we can be blinded to the truth that God has excellent gifts for us. Just ask!

Biblical principles are the basic framework for receiving those gifts. Like David, when we trust God and understand that He has our best interests at heart, it is easy to receive His gifts and allow the Holy Spirit to direct us. The leading of the Holy Spirit is like a navigation system giving us the specific direction in which we need to go.

Our heavenly Father's love for us is pure and unconditional. His love for us is not based upon performance. Our heavenly Father's unreserved love for us is one of the greatest gifts that He could give. We are able to love without limitations because He first loved us that way. Isn't it easy to give back to others who freely give first (i.e., love, forgive, care, show concern, etc.)? When we are able to receive this unconditional love from Him, it empowers us to give it to others.

> *(Alan)* My father was a great example of unconditional love. During World War II, my mother's first husband died, leaving her expecting their first child, Dixon. Later she married my father, and they had my older brother, Tommy, and me. Dixon is nine years older than I am. My father always treated us all with the same kindness and loving attitude. We never felt that he loved Dixon any less because he was not his biological father.

When Jamie and I married and purchased our first house, my father volunteered to help us paint and repair it, and those kind actions were offered by no one else. He'd done it for Dixon and his wife, Karen, as well as for Tommy and his wife, Jane. It was my father's way of showing his support and approval in celebrating our first home with us. That is just the way he has always been. Our relationship with Dad has always been a picture of how our heavenly Father loves us and is available for us.

As we understand the heart of the Father and His love for us, we are able to receive every good gift He gives. The Holy Spirit in marriage is one of those excellent gifts to be utilized and cherished.

A PRAYER FOR YOUR MARRIAGE

Dear Lord,
You are a gracious and generous, heavenly Father. We desire to be like David in knowing that "Your beauty and love chase after us every day of our lives." You are perfect in every way and know what is ultimately best for us. Thank You for Your unconditional love and for the gift of the Holy Spirit who leads and directs us. We want every good gift that You have to give. We desire to draw nearer to You so that we will know the heart of the Father.

Chapter Five

Known of Him

(Jamie) I remember the first time I listened to a tape a friend gave me on how the Father would talk about me. It was a man's voice speaking in authority, yet was kind and honoring at the same time. I imagined my heavenly Father was talking specifically to me. His words to me were so wonderfully affirming that I began to weep. I was in my thirties and for the first time in my life, I received revelation of the Father's adoration of me. It was a moment that I will never forget.

Keep me as the apple of Your eye; Hide me under the shadow of Your wings (Psalms 17:8 NKJ).

Have you ever meditated on what the Scriptures say about how God sees you? Did you know that according to God's Word, you ...

- Are righteous and holy (Ephesians 4:24)
- Are chosen of God, holy and dearly loved (Colossians 3:12; Thessalonians 1:4)
- Are the apple of His eye (Psalms 17:8)
- Are a member of a chosen race, a royal priesthood, a holy nation, a people for God's own possession (1 Peter 2:9-10)

- Are a holy partaker of a heavenly calling (Hebrews 3:1)
- Are a child of God who resembles Christ when He returns (1 John 3:1-2)
- Are forever free from condemnation (Romans 8:1)
- Have the mind of Christ (1 Corinthians 2:16)
- Have been blessed with every spiritual blessing (Ephesians 1:3)
- Have been redeemed and forgiven and a recipient of His lavish grace (Ephesians 1:6-8)
- Have been given the spirit of love, power, and a sound mind or self-discipline (2 Timothy 1:7)
- Have direct access to God through the Spirit (Ephesians 2:18)
- Have the right to come boldly before the throne of God to receive mercy and find grace for help in time of need (Hebrews 4:16)
- Have been given precious and magnificent promises by God, by which you are a partaker of His divine nature (2 Peter 1:4)

These promises are *so* incredibly amazing that I have a sheet of them and many more to remind me of the authority I am to walk in so that I don't thwart it. I begin to think earthly minded thoughts if I'm not careful to renew my mind with God's Word.

> *(Jamie)* I know that my God has a sense of humor, so in order to change my perception of the way I saw God, I began to see him in my mind's eye as a BIG male cheerleader with black and white saddle oxfords, a big megaphone, shorts, and an oversized letter sweater with a big green (my favorite color) "J" on it. You guessed it. I had to see God as *my* cheerleader and biggest fan, not as an imposing scary being. And to this day, I see Him as my cheerleader, encouraging me on to accomplish His best.

God thinks the absolute best of us. He sees us as *holy.* That just doesn't seem right, yet that is what He says of us in Scripture. What an amazing God we have! We need to understand how proud He is of us and how much He loves us. It is a beautiful picture of how a good father is supposed to be with his children. So even if you didn't have the best earthly father, by your knowing your heavenly Father's nature, you can break a "lack of parenting" cycle and be the parent you want your children to have. That is the beauty of having the perfect Father, God. Not that you will be the perfect parent, but through His Word and through the leading of the Holy Spirit, He will show you how to do it.

"So now Jesus and the ones he makes holy have the same Father. That is why Jesus is not ashamed to call them his brothers and sisters" (Hebrews 2:11 NLT). *Sanctified* means, "the process to make free from sin." So as we get closer to God and are more like Him, we are becoming more holy like Him. This is how we are made holy. He is not interested in the external but the internal "heart change." I've heard it said that He wants to perform heart surgery on us (maybe even a heart transplant, if necessary). When we get our hearts right, the external takes care of itself.

Psalms 139 is a wonderful psalm acknowledging the Father's total knowledge of our thoughts, words, and actions. Verse fourteen says, *"You are fearfully and wonderfully made."* Read Psalms 139 often. Let His knowledge of you settle into your spirit. The Word says that He knows how many hairs are upon your head (Matthew 10:30). *"Such knowledge is too wonderful for me; it is high, I cannot attain unto it"* (Psalms 139:6 NKJ).

Take a moment to read the entire Psalm now. It helps us to understand how awesomely big our God is. You need to see that you are God's workmanship—His handiwork (Ephesians 2:10), a one of a kind. The Master signed His masterpiece on the day you were born into this world, and all the angels rejoiced. Your creation was a celebration!

When you truly understand the Father's love for you, I am convinced that you will not be as concerned about what man thinks. You will gladly obey Him and receive His gifts of grace and mercy without hesitation.

We know that Satan is like a roaring lion trying to steal, kill, and destroy (John 10:10). There is nothing that he would like more than for us to reject God's gifts. He doesn't want us to receive God's blessing or to operate in His power and is doing everything he can to keep us from getting it. He is the father of lies, trying to distort or pervert God's truth. We have to remember, there is both the Father of truth and a father of lies out there. We must be able to distinguish between the two. It is simple enough: God—good; devil—bad.

Marriage is one of God's most prized gifts to be cherished because it is a holy and unique covenant made between man and God. God says to give honor to marriage and remain faithful to one another in marriage (Hebrews 13:4). If we have a good understanding of the way in which God sees us—holy, righteous, and chosen—it frees us to be better husbands and wives. We can be more forgiving, less judgmental, and able to overlook our mate's faults.

God says wonderful things about us—that we are righteous and holy. He wants us to believe them and allow the truth of His Word concerning us to penetrate our hearts. When we believe this to be true about ourselves, we begin to act differently towards our mate, and we become what God has said we are, thereby transforming our relationship.

The Holy Spirit helps in the transformation process by reminding us of how He sees us and who we are. In God's eyes, we have been redeemed and forgiven. He sees us as holy and righteous because of the blood of Jesus Christ. Invite the Helper, our Advocate, into your heart and see yourself as God does!

A PRAYER FOR YOUR MARRIAGE

Dear Lord,
Thank You for giving us revelation on how You see us and that You make us holy. You have said such kind things about us as Your children. Our goal is to believe they are true. We want to understand Your love for us so that we may freely give Your love and grace to others. Thank You for the transforming power of the Helper, the Holy Spirit.

Chapter Six

Heart Condition

(Jamie) When Alan and I were trying to sell our first house, we had a period of frustration. Although we had been prayerful throughout the process, we were having trouble selling it. It was an adorable starter home in a prime location. We had found a new house to buy, and we needed to sell this one.

One Sunday morning when we were getting ready for church, Alan blurted out, "We will never sell this house!" "Yes we will!" I responded. No sooner had I gotten those words out of my mouth than the phone rang. Alan answered simply saying, "OK, goodbye" and hung up. It was a young single lady who had looked at the house weeks earlier and wanted to come over that afternoon to make an offer on it.

(Jesus) "Then He spoke of many things to them in parables saying, 'Behold, a sower went out to sow. And as he sowed, some seed fell by the wayside, and the birds came and devoured them. Some fell on stony places, where they did not have much earth; and they immediately sprang up because they had no

> *depth of earth. But when the sun was up they were scorched, and because they had no root they withered away. And some fell among thorns, and the thorns sprang up and choked them. But others fell on good ground and yielded a crop; some a hundred fold, some sixty and some thirty. He who has ears to hear, let them hear!'"* (Matthew 13:3-9 NKJ).

The parable speaks of the soil and where the seeds take root. Depending on where the seed was placed, it either flourished or died. The soil represents the condition of our hearts or our ability to receive and believe God in our minds as well as in our hearts. The yield of the "crops" represents the level of faith in God to perform His Word.

> *(Alan)* That Sunday morning I had allowed my frustration to chip away at my level of faith, and it affected my heart. My heart was not good soil at that moment. Jamie, however, had not allowed the frustration of our situation to affect her. She reminded me to look at the truth of God's Word and not our current situation. Our situation changed in an instant because she remained strong in faith.

God had been at work behind the scenes all along. Just because we did not see what He was doing did not mean that He was not involved. He moved immediately to dispel any doubt or unbelief that was trying to surface. We tangibly felt the presence of God in the room at that very moment.

We need to remain steadfast and strong for each other, especially when the other is weak. We don't want or even like having those weak moments. God does not like faithlessness either. He uses the words *wicked* and *perverted* in speaking of faithlessness in Matthew 17:17, Mark 9:19, and Luke 9:41. That is how strongly He feels about it.

We are to be active participants in faith by not just speaking with our mouths but also believing in our hearts as well. Faith man, Smith Wigglesworth, commonly said, "Only believe" because he saw unbelief as the greatest stumbling block in our faith walk. Mark 11:24 (AMP) says, *"Whatever you ask for in prayer, believe that it is granted to you, and you will get it."*

> *(Alan)* On a company trip several years ago, Jamie and I were at a resort in Mexico along with the president of the company and his wife. While talking one afternoon, they mentioned flying separately to the resort. They proceeded to tell us that when they traveled by air, they always traveled in separate planes—one parent with one child and one parent with the other. We asked why they did that. They explained that in case there was a plane crash, half of the family would survive.

Instead of seeing family vacations as a wonderful opportunity to build faith, they were planting seeds of fear in their children's hearts. Before a trip, we always pray together as a family, asking God to protect us from any incident. We plead Psalms 91 (the prayer of protection) over our vacation time and plead the blood of Jesus over us as a family. Then we go and have a great time in peace, knowing that our God will protect us. We are also careful to listen to Him to know how and when to proceed with our plans.

Anyone who gardens knows that the soil must be properly prepared. The seeds need water and sunlight to grow. The weeds must be removed, or they will choke out the new growth. Our relationship with God is like the garden. The soil, being our hearts, needs to be prepared with daily prayer and the reading of God's Word, which is the water and sunlight that grow our relationship with Him. Removing the weeds keeps a worldly perspective from corrupting a godly perspective.

In other words, instead of thinking that we may die on vacation, we need to understand that God is protecting us, and there is no need to worry. We are so bombarded with the world's perspective that we must be careful not to get desensitized to what we know as believers. The Bible directs us in our thinking to mediate on whatever things are true, noble, just and pure, lovely, of good report, of any virtue, and praiseworthy (Philippians 4:8).

Without the help of the Holy Spirit, we can so easily fall prey to the sin of negative thinking or speaking critical words over a person, situation, or even our own marriages. The Bible says that out of the abundance of the heart the mouth speaks (Matthew 12:34 AMP). In other words, how we truly feel eventually comes out of our mouth. Without the accountability of our spouses, we could head down that slippery slope. We need to be honest with ourselves about our perspective. We must fight that sinful nature.

Years ago, there was a national pastor's conference being held, drawing many recognized church leaders. At the opening of the meeting, the pastors were asked to take a moment to pray to prepare their hearts before starting. As they did this, they began to hear someone weeping. It escalated to the point that the others began to look around to see who the sinner was. As the prayer time came to a close, everyone realized the weeping man to be the Reverend Billy Graham. As one of our nations most trusted leaders, this godly man understood the sinful condition of man's heart. In his humility, he saw God as his sole sufficiency. He was dependent on the power of the Holy Spirit as his Counselor. Billy Graham's heart is good soil that God has used to produce a hundredfold return. We too need to focus on our hearts being good soil and think on whatever things are true, noble, etc.

A PRAYER FOR YOUR MARRIAGE

Dear Lord,
We invite the Holy Spirit, our Helper, to reveal to us the mysteries of the kingdom. We want Your Word to flourish in our hearts and our faith to grow. Help us to maintain a faith filled and strong heart condition. "Create in me a pure heart, O God, And renew a steadfast spirit within me" (Psalms 51:10 NKJ). "Make us strong and perfect, fully confident of the whole will of God" (Colossians 4:12). Help us to have hearts that are good soil that will produce a hundredfold return.

Chapter Seven

Prayer POWer

(Jamie) From the early days of our marriage, I often prayed for Alan. But I remember the first time Alan came to me asking for prayer over a work related situation. I felt honored by his request because this showed me that he really valued my prayers. We progressed to praying for each other aloud and for other matters as they related to our lives together. We were strengthened in our spirits through agreement and in our marriage relationship because we trusted each another enough to be vulnerable through prayer. James 5:16 (AMP) says the earnest, heartfelt, and continued prayer of a righteous man makes tremendous power available, dynamic in its working.

Prayer is the secret of power (Evan Roberts, Welsh revivalist).

Praying together was a major advancement in our marriage relationship and in our faith walk. We began to see the hand of God move mightily and quicker than when we had prayed independently. There is power in corporate prayer. More powerful than corporate prayer, however, are the prayers of husbands and wives praying together.

Because marriage is God ordained, He places great power in the relationship. We unlock this great force through agreement in prayer. As we grow in our relationship with God, we begin to have the mind of Christ. The prayer for ourselves is that we would not seek our own desires, but to seek for ourselves what God wants.

Prayer is the single most interactive form of communication available to us where we can directly call forth God's power and presence. Wow! Ever thought of prayer in quite that way? It is an awesome concept. All we have to do is whisper His name, and He is there. When we taught a Sunday school class of teenagers, we told them that when they called, God's phone was never busy, and they would never have to leave a message. He is always right there.

There is a great series of books by Stormie O'Martian on prayer. Two of our favorites are *The Power of a Praying Husband* and *The Power of a Praying Wife*. In the first chapter of Stormie's book, *The Power of a Praying Wife*, she confesses her initial prayer was asking God to "change him." She admits she needed God to change her heart towards her husband so that she would pray earnest prayers for him. The beauty of these books is that they are topical. The Table of Contents lists certain topics you may choose to pray about for your spouse.

For example, if a wife wanted to pray for her husband in the area of work, she would find the topic listed under "His Work." In the text there will be a personal example of something Stormie experienced as it relates to her spouse's work. Then, there is a prayer based on Scripture with blanks so that you can insert your spouse's name. Then in the last part of the chapter, there is a listing of Scriptures that you can claim over your spouse. It is a wonderful resource. We recommend it often because there are so many couples we meet with who do not pray with or for their spouse. When meeting with couples, we require them to obtain these books and read and pray these prayers together in order to help develop their personal prayer dialog.

(Jamie) I remember one morning when I first got the book, *The Power of a Praying Wife*, I picked it up, looked at the Table of Contents, and asked the Holy Spirit what I needed to pray for Alan that day. I slid my finger down the list of topics and was led to the "His Work" prayer for Alan that day. When he arrived home, he began to share with me how he could see that every job he had had in his professional career had prepared him for what he was currently doing. He had even recently gotten involved with the Germany Partnership, a professional organization of German companies, which he was enjoying and through which he was making new business contacts. Alan had taken three years of German in high school and had been the state representative for the German club his senior year.

The prayer for that day had stated, "Give him enough confidence in the gifts You've placed in him to be able to seek, find, and do good work. Open doors of opportunity for him that no man can close. Develop his skills so that they grow more valuable with each passing year." I could see how the Holy Spirit had led me to the perfect prayer for him that day in encouraging him.

Soon I was praying my own tailor-made prayers for Alan. It was an amazing feeling to be working hand in hand with God for my husband through prayer. When Alan saw how powerfully it worked for him, he bought *The Power of a Praying Husband* for himself. He keeps it in his briefcase so that he can pray for me during the day. It was something he wanted to do for me, which I value immensely.

The Bible says that we are to pray without ceasing. That means we are to have an ongoing conversation with God throughout our days. He created us for His good pleasure. He enjoys time with us. He longs for relationship with us. If we have good communion with Him first, then we can have the mind of Christ so that we pray His will (not our will) through our prayers. Wouldn't it be a beautiful thing if His wisdom flowed directly down from heaven into our prayers, as if conduits, influencing the world around us? That is how it is *supposed* to work. We challenge you to pray together and watch what God does!

Our spouse should be the recipient of this outpouring of God's wisdom through our prayers. Likewise, we should be the recipient of our spouse's outpouring of wisdom. If we both are children of God, this should be the case. Out of our love and concern for each other comes a desire for us to see our spouse complete and content. In Bible times, when the Jewish people were greeted, "How are you?" they responded, "Shalom," which means, "nothing broken, nothing missing, complete." Prayer is the empowerment we have as Christians to participate in that process of completion and contentment with our spouse. *"Therefore confess your sins to each other and pray for each other so that you may be healed. The prayer of a righteous man/woman is powerful and effective"* (James 5:16 NIV).

There is tremendous power in the marriage relationship where prayer is concerned. Because it is God's ordained and blessed way for us to live, our prayers together have a special authority based upon the relationship between husband and wife. *"I tell you that if two of you on earth agree about anything you ask for, it will be done for you by my Father in heaven"* (Matthew 18:19 NIV). Praying together is a part of our marriage relationship that we cherish the most. There is closeness through spiritual intimacy that is difficult to put into words.

(Alan) Our son was diagnosed as having a learning disability while in the second grade. We knew something was

not right with his spelling and writing ability. Later we learned it was called *dysgraphia*, a disorder that affected his ability to process information on paper.

Jamie and I began to pray together, daily agreeing and believing for James to be healed of dysgraphia. We were careful never to speak of him as being learning disabled. We would pray specifically asking God to correct the problem and speak words of life over James as if he were already healed. For example, we would pray that James had the mind of Christ and was fully able to function, understand, and excel in all his subjects. We thanked God for the work that He was doing in James' mind.

The next year when James was tested in school, his scores showed marked improvement. We rejoiced over the progress; however, God was not finished. When tested each year, his scores continued to improve. By the time he was in high school, he was scoring in the gifted range and was taking advanced placement courses. During his senior year he was in a college level Western Civics course making an A! He is now in his first year at the University of Alabama, Birmingham (as a student of nursing). We were just notified that he qualifies to be in their Honor Society. God had heard and responded to our desperate prayers.

You may feel uncomfortable, self-conscious, or even intimidated at first by praying aloud with your spouse. But we would like to challenge you to let your barriers down and persevere, easing into it. You don't have to pray long, fancy prayers. Just pray from your heart. Start out simply, and as you get more comfortable, pray more specifically. The Holy Spirit will show us how to pray and will reveal to us the things we need to know. All we need to do is ask Him. *"Let us approach the throne of grace with confidence, so that we may receive mercy and find grace to help us in our time of need"* (Hebrews 4:16 NIV).

Prayer is a spiritual intimacy that blesses marriage immensely. It promises to share a facet of our spouse that we will want to experience more. The Third Cord binds us together in spiritual intimacy with God and our spouse. Prayer power strengthens the Three Fold Cord. Alan and I fell even more in love with each other when we practiced this often untapped form of intimacy together. Pray together often without ceasing!

A PRAYER FOR YOUR MARRIAGE

Dear Lord,
You are always available for us. You are faithful, oh God, as the Third Cord that binds our marriage together. We desire to have prayer intimacy in our marriage relationship. We invite the Holy Spirit into our prayer life. Thank you that You sent the Helper to show us a better way to do things. Reveal to us the power of prayer through the leading of the Holy Spirit. Make it easy and not hard for us. Thank You for the power available to us through praying in agreement. Father, help make us mindful to pray together often.

Chapter Eight

God Power

(Jamie) God speaks to us through Scripture, but He is an immensely creative God who uses a multitude of ways to communicate with us (through the Holy Spirit, other believers, dreams, visions, situations, circumstances, and Scripture). We need discernment in order to know when God is trying to speak or communicate with us in these unique ways. When we do experience it, we need to understand what God is trying to tell us.

God is far more than can be measured, described, defined in ordinary language, or pinned down to any particular happening. —David Jenkins

(Alan) I recall a story from John Wimber's book, *Power Evangelism*. Upon boarding a plane, he encountered a man who had a woman's name supernaturally superimposed on his forehead. The man appeared to be traveling with his wife. John realized that God was telling him that this gentleman was having an affair with the woman whose name was on his forehead. John had an opportunity on the flight to confront this man privately.

This man knew it was God or how else would a total stranger have known this about him. God showed John to tell this man that if he did not come clean with his wife regarding his sin immediately, then his life would be taken prematurely. This information was taken to heart by the gentleman, and he dealt with it right away. Now *this* is supernatural!

(Jamie) When our son, James, was a young boy, he began running a high fever during the night. Alan and I were both home but were totally exhausted from differing busy and late night schedules. We were no doubt sleeping soundly. Because James' room was downstairs and ours was upstairs, we were unable to hear him. During the night, he had come up and put a palette on our bedroom floor to sleep on, which we were accustomed to him doing. In the early morning hours, I awoke to the sound of our son's continuous hand clapping.

As he was on Alan's side of the bed, I woke up Alan to check on James. Alan told me that he was sound asleep. Upon touching him, however, Alan could tell that James had a very high fever. We scrambled out of bed quickly to take care of his condition. After we had done so and James was awake, we asked him if he knew that he had been clapping while he was asleep. He responded that God had told him, as he slept, that we were very tired that night. He instructed him to begin clapping to wake us because he was running a high fever and needed our help. So while sleeping, he began clapping to awaken us. Alan and I looked at each other, marveling at how God had intervened on our behalf. Then James said, "And you know what they say, 'If you're happy and you know, it clap your hands.'"

The reason some Christians experience the supernatural power of God is because they are aware of its availability to them. And they take those most important actions—they *ask* the Holy Spirit for guidance and *listen* to what He has to say. We remind ourselves constantly that the Holy Spirit is available to us and wants to help if only we will ask. That is one of the many ways that Christianity is different from other religions. The *power* of God is available to us through the Holy Spirit in order to experience God's manifest power!

> *(Jamie)* I remember the first time my best friend, Mittie McCarty, shared with me a supernatural experience she'd had. I told her, "I want those kinds of experiences too." And she responded, "You can! It's there for the asking." For me, learning of the wonderful ways in which God communicates with and through us was a new concept to me. I had never heard it taught or had its availability explained to me before.

For those of us who are practical to the nth degree, we get hindered by our own minds in trying to comprehend the move of God. In other words, we cannot wrap our brains around the concept of the supernatural. I often notice people not giving credit to God or the Holy Spirit when God's miraculous deeds are passed off as simply a coincidence. We often won't allow ourselves to believe that God has intervened. "It is the heart that experiences God, not the reason" (Blaise Pascal).

We often respond in situations without inquiring of God first. We may think that it is obvious what we need to do without first asking, "Father, what do you want me to do?" People might rationalize this by saying, "Well, God has given me a good, logical mind to make these types of decisions. He knows how He made me to be." But we must be willing to submit to His leading. The most important thing to God is that we are willing to submit or accept His ways no matter how it looks.

There is a story of an American soldier separated from his unit on a Pacific island during WWII. As he scrambled for cover, he hid in one of many small caves on a high ridge. Safe for the moment, he realized the enemy soldiers were searching close behind and if they found him, he would be killed. He prayed a prayer asking God to protect him, and the soldier expressed his love and trust in Him.

After his prayer, he saw a spider crawling over the mouth of the cave covering the entrance with a web. As he watched the spider spin strand upon strand of the web, he could hear the enemy approaching. The soldier thought, *The Lord has sent me a spider web when what I need is a brick wall. God does have a sense of humor.* As he watched the enemy draw near, searching one cave after another, he prepared to make his last stand. But to his amazement, after glancing in the direction of the cave, the enemy proceeded without entering the cave.

Suddenly, the American soldier realized that the spider web over the entrance made his cave appear as if no one had entered for quite a while. "Lord, forgive me," the young man prayed, "I had forgotten that in You, a spider's web is stronger than a brick wall."

Often God does things differently from the way we think they should be done. Our job is to submit our thoughts to His thoughts even though we don't completely understand what He is trying to do for us. His ways are higher than our ways.

> *My thoughts are completely different from yours, says the Lord. And my ways are far beyond anything you could imagine. For just as the heavens are higher than the earth, so are My ways higher than yours, and My thoughts than your thoughts* (Isaiah 55:8-9).

When God is allowed to work in our lives, it increases our faith. "The way to see Faith is to shut the eye of Reason" (Ben Franklin).

The Holy Spirit sometimes manifests Himself in specific ways such as the spirit of reconciliation (restoration) and the spirit of truth (righteousness). The spirit of reconciliation is a supernatural restoration of a relationship. An example of this would be a sudden, inexplicable (being a God thing) change of heart towards someone.

The spirit of truth brings about a response of holiness and righteousness The spirit of truth may remind us of a certain Scripture relating to how we are to treat our spouse when a breech has taken place between us. An example of this might be having an argument with our spouse where we feel we are in the right. Then we have a sudden change of heart (being a God thing), experiencing the conviction that comes from the Holy Spirit and realizing that we were wrong. Second Corinthians 5:19 (AMP) says,

> *It was God [personally present] in Christ, reconciling and restoring the world to favor with Himself, not counting up and holding against [men] their trespasses [but canceling them], and committing to us the message of reconciliation (of the restoration to favor).*

We once counseled a couple in which the wife had had multiple affairs over a period of years stemming from abuse as a child. We were asked by our pastor to help them work through the past issues leading up to the affairs. She was sincerely repentant, and there were children involved. There was concern that upon learning of the most recent affair, her husband would leave her.

We told him that even though he had every right to leave, if he would submit his will to God's will, he would see a miraculous healing take place in their marriage. She was desperate to be free of her unfaithful behavior towards her husband. God used his obedience and submission to God's will to help her get free from the past. This is what God wants us to be able to do with one another.

In this case it would be *"God [personally present] in Christ* (and in you as a Christian), *reconciling and restoring, not holding against anyone their trespasses and committing to the message of reconciliation"* (2 Corinthians 5:19 (AMP). Can you think of someone with whom reconciliation seems impossible for you to accomplish? Is it your spouse? With God's manifest power of love, it *is* possible in any relationship.

I love to read "Ask Marilyn" by newspaper columnist Marilyn vos Savant. She claims the achievement of having the world's highest IQ. Her column caught my eye when a question was asked about marriage. The question was, "I often read that it takes constant work to have a good marriage. What kind of work makes sense? I don't see why marriage to a person who is right for you (and vice versa) should require continual effort."

Marilyn responded, "I believe you should always work toward these two goals: 1) overcoming your own weaknesses; but 2) allowing your spouse to have them."

Without realizing it, Marilyn was describing the spirit of reconciliation that is at work within a marriage relationship if both husband and wife are working toward these two goals. We will become better people and avoid damaging our love relationship in the process. Why is this important? Because all of us are far from perfect—even the person we marry—and if we don't learn this before the wedding, both of us will surely discover it afterward. Marriages, like the people in them, are not perfect and take work.

Poet great Auden profoundly stated, "Love each other or perish." These are powerfully stated words of wisdom on living life with our spouse. In other words, if you can not *truly love*, then why bother living? When we walk in the Spirit, we are living examples. Being empowered by the Holy Spirit, the fruit in our lives is God's unconditional love. God's transforming power is available to us if we only ask!

A PRAYER FOR YOUR MARRIAGE

Dear Lord,
We ask the Helper for guidance and understanding. Thank You that You desire for us to experience more of Your power. Help us to submit our will to Your will so that Your thoughts would become our thoughts. We pray that as we submit our ways that we will see Your power manifested in our lives. Thank You for Your promise to never leave us nor forsake us.

Chapter Nine

Balancing Act

(Alan) Several years ago, I traveled on a business trip to Oklahoma City from Birmingham. It was springtime, sunny, and really quite warm in Birmingham that morning. Arriving at the airport, I was relieved to find that my plane was there and on time. As I boarded and took my seat, ready for a quick flight having a busy day ahead with a tight time schedule, the flight attendant informed us that we were not leaving anytime soon.

She explained that our plane had come from Chicago where it was cold and snowy. During the flight, ice had accumulated on the wings, and we needed to have the plane de-iced. Well, since Birmingham had no de-icing equipment, the solution was to sit and wait while the sun melted the ice from the wings. After about an hour and a half of de-icing, we were able to take off for Dallas where I was to connect with a flight to Oklahoma City.

The delay in Birmingham meant that I would miss my connection in Dallas. And I really needed to be in Oklahoma City on time that day. In flight I was reading my Bible and praying. I read John 16:24, *"Until now you have asked for nothing in my name; ask and you will receive, that your joy may be made full."* I asked God to let me get to Oklahoma City on time, whatever it took. It was one of the first times that I asked God specifically to do something for me.

As we approached Dallas, the flight attendant begin calling out the connecting flights and gate numbers for the passengers on my flight. After several moments she was finished, but she had provided no connection information for my flight to Oklahoma City. After a brief pause she mentioned, as if it was no big deal, that if anyone were going to Oklahoma City, this would be his or her flight. She said, "We'll just make a quick stop here in Dallas to drop off passengers and then be on our way."

She explained that my connecting flight had mechanical problems and was grounded so the airline had reassigned this plane to go directly to Oklahoma City. I thought to myself, *Way to go, God!* What a supernatural and creative way to get me there on time; I was on the right flight all along and would not be troubled with changing planes!

The supernatural *does* exist. That day on the airplane, I experienced the supernatural power of God. We can allow ourselves to be talked out of believing in a supernatural occurrence because it cannot be explained in the natural. We need to balance our knowledge of Scripture with a belief in the supernatural power of God.

Like a balance scale, we need to balance the supernatural with our knowledge of Scripture. Imagine a balance scale with a bowl on each side and a bar connecting them attached to a stand. In order to be properly balanced, we need to understand and accept the supernatural power of God in one bowl. In the other bowl, we need an understanding of the Scriptures using the various versions of the Bible, concordances, commentaries, which are examples of natural resources to help us understand God and God's Word better. According to *Webster's New World Dictionary*, *supernatural* is defined as "of an order of existence outside the natural world; attributed to divine power."

We often have difficulty grasping the supernatural because it originates outside of the natural realm and cannot be proven with tangible evidence. We can ask the Holy Spirit to enlighten us and interpret the Scriptures for us to gain more understanding. The *supernatural* is understood by the spirit of man. The *natural* is understood by the mind. Balancing the natural with the supernatural allows us to experience God more powerfully. In the natural, we could see that our son was having difficulty with dysgraphia; however, in the supernatural realm, we knew that the power of God was available to heal him. As we agreed in prayer for his total restoration, we believed the healing Scriptures in the Bible and spoke them over him daily. As mentioned in the previous chapter, we experienced the supernatural healing power of God over his situation.

Do you remember when the disciple Thomas said, *"Unless I see His hands the print of the nails, and put my finger in the print of the nails, and put my hand into his side, I will not believe"* (John 20:25 NKJV). Thomas, who had seen Jesus perform many miracles, who had been with him when He raised Lazarus from the dead, would not believe that Jesus had returned after His death unless he could *see* with his own eyes. Jesus' first words after greeting the disciples, after His resurrection, were directed towards Thomas.

He said, *"Reach your finger here, and look at My hands, and reach your hand here, and put it into my side. Do not be unbelieving, but believing"* (John 20:27 NKJV). Ouch! Don't you know that hurt Thomas, coming from Jesus? Making His point, Jesus said to

Thomas, *"Because you have seen Me, you have believed. Blessed are those who have not seen and yet believed"* (John 20:29 NKJV).

This example about Thomas is in God's Word for our benefit. We are called to know there *is* a spirit realm, to acknowledge it, welcome it, embrace it, exercise it, and trust it. It could save your life. A Bible study teacher once told me that every time she heard a siren of an emergency vehicle, she would send up a prayer for those involved. I remember thinking, *Now that is proactive.* So from that point on when I heard one, no matter who I was with, I would take a moment to pray. My children were often in the car with me, so we would do this together.

> *(Jamie)* Once our family was on a trip to Destin, Florida, and we were going out to dinner. A terrible accident had just occurred in front of a bank. There was a car that was so flattened in the front that it looked impossible to have any survivors, but we prayed for any occupants of the car. For months, the Lord brought pictures of that accident to mind along with the thoughts of the driver. I would pray, but I remember thinking, *I don't even think that this person could have survived.* Still, I would pray. About six months later, I was talking to a woman at my church, and she told me of this school teacher friend from the Homewood School system who was in this horrific accident in Destin, Florida. She told of how her friend had gone to an ATM machine for some cash at dinnertime, and how this accident had almost taken her life.
>
> After a long recovery, she went back to her elementary teaching job where she would impact many young lives. As the date, time, and location had been confirmed, I *knew* it was the accident we had seen. God is faithful to reward *our* faithfulness. When I think back on how this even came up

in our conversation, I can't recall. All I know is that God made a way for us to find out because He wanted us to know that our prayers were heard and honored. To this day, I tell my children when we hear a siren, you never know, you may be praying for the life of your future spouse.

There are a couple of great application books on the manifest power of God by Jack Deere. They are: *Surprised by the Voice of God* and *Surprised by the Power of the Spirit*. These books contain many practical examples, some that even describe a matter of life and death. In one story, Jack tells of a dream his wife had regarding their daughter's imminent danger from a stranger intent on killing her. His wife's dream was confirmed by two other sources. This prompted much prayer over their daughter for protection. As they took precautions to safeguard her in the natural, she received supernatural protection. No harm came to their daughter because of their understanding of the supernatural protection of God.

In a recent article, a pastor compared a Christian's experience with God to that of a whitewater rafting adventure. He said either you can ride the gentle waves, or you can experience an exciting, exhilarating ride. Your choice will impact eternity. Our thirteen-year-old daughter, Hayden, recently asked a profound question: "If we are supposed to live life on earth and be close to God, how can we do that in this world (carnal place)?" We told her it was like walking a tightrope, balancing between the natural and the supernatural. We must stay spiritually sensitive and pure amid the wrong thought patterns and sin around us. We must renew our minds. *"If the godly compromise with the wicked, it is like polluting a fountain or muddying a spring"* (Proverbs 25:26 NLT).

"Do not be conformed any longer to the pattern of the world but be transformed by the renewing of your mind" (Romans 12:2 NIV). We can get so bogged down by the day-to-day problems that we lose

sight of heavenly possibilities. In some ways, it is like thinking outside the box. It is thinking on what God *can* do instead of what *can't* happen in the natural.

> *(Alan)* As in the airplane experience, I could not *see* any reason for what happened. I simply had to trust in God and believe that He would get me to my destination on time. God is our hope in seemingly hopeless situations. He always makes a way where there seems to be no way.

Now that we understand the *supernatural* (Holy Spirit, spirit of reconciliation, spirit of truth) and the *natural* (experiences and resources available to help us better understand God and His Word), we see how they have different functions. Combining the two different manifestations of the Holy Spirit enriches the Christian experience.

A PRAYER FOR YOUR MARRIAGE

Dear Lord,
Help us to balance the natural with the supernatural. Please help us be sensitive to the ways in which You communicate with us. We want to experience Your power working around and through us so that we may partner with You. We need greater understanding of You, the Helper, the One who is called beside. It is our desire to walk in Your power every day of our lives.

Chapter Ten

R-E-S-P-E-C-T

> *(Jamie)* Our son, James, and daughter, Hayden, had a wise third grade teacher who went over the classroom rules at the first of the year. I remember them telling me that the "Golden Rule" was rule number one: "Do unto others as you would have them do unto you." It is good to keep it in the forefront of your mind or on the tablet of your heart, so that you treat others in a way that you yourself would like to be treated—with *respect*.

Aretha Franklin sings a popular song about respect. In it she asks that *he* find out what kind of treatment *she* prefers. If you have ever heard Aretha Franklin sing this song, you can tell that she is passionate about respect. That is what all people want—to be respected. Generally speaking, respectful behavior is described similarly by most people. *Webster's New World Dictionary* defines respect as, "to feel or show honor, or esteem for, to consider or treat with deference or dutiful regard"; "to show consideration for, avoid intruding upon or interfering with; and "to concern, or relate to."

> *Husbands, love your wives, just as Christ loved the church and gave himself up for her* (Ephesians 5:25).

> *Even so husbands should love their wives as [being in a sense] their own bodies. He who loves his own wife loves himself. For no man ever hated his own flesh, but nourishes it as Christ does the church* (Ephesians 5:28-29 AMP).

The greatest desire a wife has of her husband is that he unselfishly love her and put her well-being before his own desires. Just as Christ sacrificed His own life for the church, Jesus calls us to a higher standard by telling husbands to love their wives as Christ loved the church. He also called husbands to love their wives as their own flesh. A man who loves or takes proper care of his physical body (gets the required exercise, balanced diet, and doesn't abuse his body in any way) should love his wife with the same diligence.

In his relationship with his wife, he is to nourish and care for her as he would himself. As we are living in a very image conscious society, we see many people invest much time and money on their bodies. They may become out of balance in their commitment by putting more emphasis on being physically fit than working on personal relationships. Ephesians 5:33 AMP says,

> *Let the wife see that she respects, reverences her husband [that she notices him, regards him, honors him, prefers him, venerates and esteems him, and that she defers to him, praises him, loves and admires him exceedingly].*

The way in which these words are used almost seems like worship, doesn't it? It is in effect an act of worship when you treat your husband as God instructs you to do. This passage gives women the key to how their spouses are wired emotionally. Men need to have their wives praise and esteem them, to respect and honor them, and to show reverence for them.

> *(Alan)* When I have completed a long day at the office or a long "honey do" list at home, it makes me feel great for Jamie to recognize my accomplishments. Men need to feel valued by their wives. They will be willing to move mountains for their wives if this scriptural advice is taken to heart.

> The Bible addresses the wife's influence in 1 Peter 3:2 AMP,

> *When they* (husbands) *observe the pure and modest way in which you* (wives) *conduct yourselves together with your reverence [for your husband; you are to feel for him all that reverence includes: to respect, to defer, to revere him—to honor, esteem, appreciate, prize, and in the human sense, to adore him, that is to admire, praise, be devoted to, deeply love, and enjoy your husband].*

There is a reason why these same words keep showing up when talking of marriage: respect, love, esteem, reverence, and honor. These actions are necessary to a good marriage. Take note that in God's infinite wisdom, He is telling wives and husbands just how influential each of their roles is in the marriage relationship. God is saying, "OK, I want you to get this. This is important." Our attitude towards our spouse is key to the response we get from them. This spouse of ours needs to know that we really like them.

God goes to such great lengths to make this point because He knows there will be a good return on it. If He takes time to address it, it is because He needs us to "get it." It is for our good and for the good of the marriage relationship. If we will listen to the voice of the Holy Spirit, He will instruct and guide us in applying these important scriptural truths.

We may be thinking to ourselves that our spouse does not deserve our respect or love; however, that is not what God's Word says. Husbands are to love their wives, and wives are to respect their husbands, according to Ephesians 5:33. If we will make the decision to obey His Word and commit it to prayer, then He will bless our efforts. We challenge you to acknowledge all of your spouse's good characteristics and let them know that you appreciate those qualities. That will help motivate your spouse to work on their weaknesses. Your spouse knows their negative characteristics anyway. Pointing them out doesn't usually help. Affirmation can transform a person into the "new and improved" version.

Remember when Sally Field won the Academy Award after years of working in the industry. She began on the small screen and eventually graduated to films, receiving the ultimate award from her peers—the Academy Award. She caught a lot of flack for the honest, heartfelt words of her acceptance speech. "You *really* like me!" was her response in receiving the affirmation, appreciation, and respect from her peers. Affirmation of our spouse is a must, both publicly and privately.

We counseled a couple who were not doing well in their relationship. We will never forget what he said in a moment of vulnerability and frustration. "Tell her to treat me right!" Do you hear what he was saying? He was saying, "I need my wife to respect me." A marriage will certainly have its moments. However, even in a disagreement with a spouse, you can agree to disagree respectfully.

> *(Jamie)* I had wonderful parents and a good home life. Something I noticed early on about marital communication between my parents was that when they had a disagreement, certain behaviors (harsh words, sarcasm) became unproductive. My mother would be the first to say, "I don't like the way you are talking to me." She didn't stuff her feelings. She clearly let my father know when they had

strayed beyond where they needed to go in order to accomplish a resolution. In other words she was saying, "We digress." They usually didn't argue in front of us. However, there were times, like when we were together in a car, where privacy was not an option. This was a healthy way for me to see effective conflict resolution between husband and wife. Both of my parents are direct, so they usually got to the point quickly. My parents shared a mutual respect for one another.

In having a disagreement, we should take turns expressing ourselves while actively listening to the other person. No one should resort to harsh words. Take a minute to think before speaking. When we are angry, we may say something we wish we hadn't that can never be erased from the memory of our loved one. In conflict resolution, we should avoid using exaggerations (*you never* or *you always*).

(Jamie) I am not proud of this example that I am about to share with you, but it shows how you can get so focused on doing something that you can tune out people's feelings. The Holy Spirit showed me one day that I was being rude to Alan. After a hard day in the office, he would arrive home. I would be preparing dinner and would say "Hello" over my shoulder to him without leaving my spot by the cooktop. Now when he comes in, I put down whatever I am doing (be it cooking or talking on the phone), greet him with a kiss, and chat a minute before going back to dinner preparations.

The Helper showed me that Alan needed my undivided attention just for that moment. When I stopped to think about how it would make me feel to be treated the same

> way I had treated him, I realized how wrong it was. It sounds so simple, but it made a big difference in our relationship. I had always been glad for him to be home, but he didn't know it by my actions. Now he feels that he was missed and appreciated, not like a distraction to my meal preparation. Do you see the difference? Falling into taking your spouse for granted is easy if you aren't careful. Quality time is one of Alan's main love languages. (We discuss love languages later in the book.)

Vincent van Gogh once said, "Great things are not done by impulse alone, but by a series of small things brought together." Having a successful marriage is a "great thing" to accomplish because it is not always easy to stick with something when it gets difficult. It is much easier to leave a bad marriage. But the problem is that we will have never worked through the issues that caused our difficulties in the first place, and it will be unresolved for the potential next person. "A series of small things that are brought together" is persevering through those aggravations and discovering what works, with the intent to succeed.

We must be intentional in our expression of respect and love for our spouse. Ephesians clearly states that wives are called to *respect* their husbands, and husbands are to *love* their wives as Christ loves the church. God offers wise counsel through these Scriptures. The Holy Spirit, as our advocate, will remind us of the words that Jesus spoke regarding love and respect. The Third Cord will show us how to accomplish this to strengthen the marriage relationship.

A PRAYER FOR YOUR MARRIAGE

(Husband) Dear Lord,
Thank You for the gift of the Holy Spirit, who reminds me of the importance of truly respecting (wife's name) in our marriage relationship. Help me to love her truly as Christ loved the church and gave Himself up for her. Holy Spirit, show me how to love her as my own body and provide for her physical and emotional well-being. I confess the times in the past when I have not treated (wife's name) as I should and ask you to make our relationship whole again. Help me to understand fully Your standard for loving her well. Thank You that as I ask, I receive from You.

(Wife) Dear Lord,
Thank You for the gift of the Holy Spirit, who reminds me of the importance of truly respecting (husband's name) in our marriage relationship. Help me to show him that I respect him and reverence him. Holy Spirit, show me how to be more mindful of noticing him, regarding him, honoring him, preferring him, esteeming him, and deferring to him, that I would admire him exceedingly. Show me how to give generously of myself to (husband's name). I confess the times in the past when I have not treated him as I should and ask You to make our relationship whole again. Help me to understand fully Your standard for loving him well. Thank You that as I ask, I receive from You.

Chapter Eleven

The Three A's

(Jamie) Have you ever been around a couple where one honestly didn't seem to appreciate the other? They would be sarcastic, ugly, or critical of their spouse publicly. That is sad and quite unfortunate. I remember noticing this about certain couples long before I was ever married, thinking, *I never want my husband to be like that with me. I want him to be my best friend and someone with whom I joyfully spend time.* And I'm pleased to say that my husband is that for me. We share one another's acceptance, approval, and affection.

Joyce Meyers once said, "One of the ways we humble ourselves is by accepting someone the way they are."

(Jamie) This quote spoke volumes to me about the relationship between Alan and me. I used to think that when he did something I didn't agree with, I was supposed to tell him. In reality, the harder thing to do would be to say nothing, accepting him as he is. We have discovered that marriage is truly the art of compromise. We have accepted each other's personality quirks and learned to work together for our good.

(Alan) Early in our marriage, we had quite a lot of conflict over our finances. I would balance the checkbook and become very angry, yelling at Jamie over the expenses that occurred each month. Looking back on it today, I don't know why I should have been angry since we had never developed a budget or set expectations about what we were to spend each month.

We agreed to attend a Financial Peace University small group together. When we finally sat down and developed a budget, we agreed upon our financial goals, and the conflict simply disappeared. We accepted each other's role in our marriage. I manage the finances while Jamie runs the household. Jamie no longer dreads the weekly balancing of the checkbook because she now appreciates the expertise that I have in our finances. I, in turn, appreciate Jamie's creativity with our budget, saving money whenever possible.

God accepts us all, so we should accept our spouse as well. A quote by Carl Jung states, "We cannot change anything unless we accept it. Condemnation does not liberate, it oppresses." The first step toward change is acceptance. Once we accept ourselves (and others), we open the door to change. Once Jamie and I accepted each other's roles, we were able to change the way we related to each other regarding our finances. That's all we had to do! We had come to the conclusion that things had to change and accepted the fact that we needed to go about it differently.

In Dr. Laura Schlessinger's book, *The Proper Care & Feeding of Husbands*, she states, "Men are simple creatures and very dependent on their wives for acceptance, approval, and affection. When those three A's are restored, all is well in their world."

(Jamie) I'm not sure when or how it started, but Alan and I began to take note of those little things that we did for one another. And we would thank each other. Some might say, "Why should I thank him/her for it? That is their job." Don't we like to be recognized when we've performed a task well? When I take time to tell my husband that I appreciate what he does for me (I get to stay home because he is a good provider for our family; he works hard all week long; we have a lovely home; we get to take fun trips; he does things around the house to help me out, etc.), he honestly looks at me like he loves me more than ever. When I tell him that I appreciate all he does, then he begins to notice all I do to help him. We make a good team. We appreciate each other.

The Serenity Prayer is a prayer that has been adopted by Alcoholics Anonymous as a life principle. It is also a good prayer for married couples.

Serenity Prayer

Lord grant me the serenity to accept those things I cannot change, the courage to change the things I can change, and the wisdom to know difference.

Acceptance and approval parallel one another. Usually when you have someone's acceptance, that person approves of you as well. But you don't always approve of behaviors or habits of the one you accept. For example, you could accept your husband, but not approve of his gambling.

Our approach toward our spouse is key. When that individual's behavior is unacceptable, it is best to address it out of concern for him or her and the marriage. If the conversation becomes judgmental, accusatory, or condemning, a touchy subject can easily escalate the conversation into a full-blown argument.

If the subject is not well received, it is probably because that person is in denial about having a problem or is feeling defensive and not ready to relinquish the obstacle. The best thing we can do in such a situation is to begin to pray, asking the Holy Spirit to guide us. By inviting the Holy Spirit into the situation, we have just equipped ourselves with the most powerful force in the universe for positive change.

Showing Affection

The primary thing to know about affection is that every person's needs are unique. Just because you might not need much in the form of an outward show of affection (holding hands, etc.), doesn't mean your spouse doesn't. Chances are your spouse's needs are different than yours. We need to ask our spouse if his or her needs are being fulfilled. If they are not, that person may be tempted to look outside the marriage to meet them.

> *(Jamie)* I read an excerpt from Dr. Laura Schlessinger's book (mentioned earlier) that grieved my heart. A husband asked his wife if a divorce would make her happy. Infuriated, she suspected he was having an affair. However, he thought she was involved in one because of her repeated rejection of sexual intimacy and told her so. She then realized he was right about her negative response to him. She had often stated that she "had a headache," "was too tired," or that he "only showed affection in the bedroom." He told her that he had longed to be alone with her, but it was difficult to continue asking after being rejected repeatedly. He said, "It was hard enough being rejected, but while you were at your most vulnerable—being naked—made it worse." He felt frustrated and miserable by his intense desire for her and not being able to satisfy it. He wished to be neutered like a dog to diminish his suffering. She was saddened by this confession and humbled to realize that she

had selfishly *not* been concerned with meeting his physical needs, while she in turn was perfectly content with her life as it was.

There is a great book entitled, *The Five Love Languages* by Gary Chapman that helps us to find out what speaks love to our spouse. The premise of the book is that there are five major categories that express love to a person: 1) Words of Affirmation, 2) Quality Time, 3) Receiving Gifts, 4) Acts of Service, or 5) Physical Touch. A person usually has one dominant love language. It is a wonderful tool for discovering how your spouse receives love. Theirs is probably different from yours, often causing friction because we tend to speak our own love language to our partner rather than theirs.

Men have the emotional need to see their wives desiring them. Because men are stimulated visually, the way a wife cares for and presents herself expresses love to him. A wife's emotional need is oftentimes fulfilled through good verbal communication, quality time, and physical touch. Learning your spouse's love language and how to speak it is a selfless act that reaps good rewards. Ask the Holy Spirit how to minister acceptance, approval, and affection to your spouse and watch what happens. We dare you, but beware: it can lead to . . . !

A PRAYER FOR YOUR MARRIAGE

Dear Lord,
Thank You that You accept us. Through the power of the Holy Spirit, help me to be more accepting of myself and (spouse's name) according to Your Word. Thank You that by the leading of the Holy Spirit I can know how to express acceptance, approval, and affection to (spouse's name) in the way that blesses them.

Chapter Twelve

Skeleton in the Closet

(Jamie) Forgiveness is a word that is easy to say but not always so easy to do. I have a picture in my head of some of the first serious conversations I had with my children. James is two years older than Hayden is. Oftentimes when conflict arose, I would have to kneel down between them, explaining that one had hurt the other and that they needed to say they were sorry (as if they meant it). We would also discuss the importance of the ability to forgive. It always seemed to be a difficult persuasion and today still can be in their teenage years.

"Love means never having to say you're sorry" (quote from the movie, *Love Story*).

"That's the stupidest thing I have ever heard of" (Harriet Thigpen, Jamie's mother).

(Alan) Forgiveness is not natural; it is supernatural! Let me say again, forgiveness is not natural but *supernatural.* When someone hurts me, my normal inclination is to strike back and hurt that person. Is that not what most of us want to do when we are hurt? I know it is for me most

> of the time. But as soon as those feelings come, right behind them the Holy Spirit reminds me of who I am and the response that I should have. I hear the voice of the Holy Spirit say, "Love your enemies, bless them that curse you, do good to them that hurt you, and pray for them which despitefully use you and persecute you; That you may be the children of your Father which is in heaven" (Matthew 5:44-45).

Sometimes saying "I'm sorry" can be just as difficult as the act of forgiving, yet it can be a totally liberating experience. Why? Because in both cases we are taking responsibility for our part in the matter. Admitting wrong is never easy, especially when the other party is unwilling to own up to his or her part. But that is not our responsibility. We are only responsible for ourselves. More times than not, each party has involvement—even unwillingness to forgive.

Pride gets in the way of our doing what is right. Pride is the skeleton in the closet. None of us wants to admit that it is there, but it is there waiting to haunt you. What does the Bible say about pride? It comes before the fall. Lucifer is the literal example of pride coming before the fall. Because of his pride in wanting to have a greater position, he was taken from heaven and sent to the pit of hell. In Leviticus 26:19, pride is addressed as rebellion. Our unwillingness to forgive is rebellion against God. When we refuse to forgive or say, "I am sorry," we are really saying that we know better than God does.

Proverbs 13:10 says that pride leads to arguments and advises us to be humble, take advice, and become wise. Do you want to be wise or rebellious (in God's sight)? We know what the Bible says about rebellion in Christians (it is likened to witchcraft), yet our flesh wants to dig in its heals as the last "hold out" in order to be right. Our sin nature often overrules our spirit nature, even as we become adults.

(Alan) Several years ago, I was involved in a business partnership with two other people. When I first joined the group, one of the partners had not been consulted. You know the saying "two's company, but three is a crowd." Well, I was the crowd! She came to resent my being a part of the group. We had major conflicts from day one on every issue. After a short period of time, I was asked to leave the partnership. Upon leaving, I said some harsh things to her and left in anger.

Several months after leaving, the Holy Spirit began convicting me of my wrong behavior and unforgiving attitude towards her. For several weeks, I argued with God, telling Him all the reasons why I was right to be angry. In my mind, I was saying, "But God, you don't understand all the things she did and said to me."

Finally I decided God was right—brilliant conclusion, right? It took a few days, but I worked up the courage to call her and apologize. She was very surprised to hear from me and even more surprised at what I had to say.

The moment I asked her to forgive me for the harsh words I had spoken, something inside me broke off, and I felt free from a huge burden. She immediately apologized for her role in the situation, and we were able to reconcile with each other. Today we are close friends and are business associates. The Holy Spirit truly knows what is best for us; if we will listen to His leading, He will free us from countless burdens.

(Jamie) I had a very wise mother. I remember having had hard feelings over something from earlier years (which to

> this day I cannot remember the specifics). When I finally mentioned it to her, she didn't make any excuses, she took responsibility for it. She said, "I'm sorry. That was wrong of me." I was so amazed that even as she spoke those words, the burden I'd carried for so many years seemed to melt away. It physically lifted from my very being. I immediately forgave her. It was a supernatural experience that I will never forget. That is why I believe I cannot remember the offense to this day.

Is it more important to *be right* or to have a *right relationship* with someone? That is what we need to ask ourselves next time we get into a disagreement with someone. My mother humbled herself before God and me because our relationship was more important to her. *"It is hard to stop a quarrel once it starts, so don't let it begin"* (Proverbs 17:14 TLB).

Forgiveness frees us up along with the other person (the offender). When we choose not to forgive, we are in a holding pattern in our walk with God. We can say we are Christians, but we are in bondage because of our unforgiveness. And it blocks us from the full power in which God wants us to operate. In other words, we are not functioning on all four cylinders.

There is great spiritual power in forgiveness. This is an incredible gift to give someone. Have you ever known someone to be a gracious forgiver? When I think of an example of this, I think of Stephen. As he was being stoned, he said, "Lord, do not charge them with this death." Many believe that *this* statement allowed God to use Saul (Paul), the one who guarded the clothes of those stoning Stephen. Saul's destiny was transformed by Stephen's forgiveness of him. Do you see that our willingness to forgive can change the destiny of our relationship with others?

Reinhold Neibuhr was quoted as saying, "Forgiveness is the final form of love."

> *(Jamie)* I know during ministry time when individuals would come up feeling as if their communication and relationship with God were being hindered, Alan or I would often ask if there was any unforgiveness in their lives. Sometimes people acted offended with this question. However, those sincere about getting to the source would humble themselves and try to consider that possibility without hesitation.

Some people *think* they have forgiven someone, but often the enemy is behind the scenes reminding them of the pain from the past. As a result, unforgiveness creeps back in their lives. Oftentimes we must forgive over and over again for the same point of contention that we thought that we had already forgiven. Forgiveness is a process. We are complex in our issues. Like an onion, there are layers of pain within us. The good Lord knows that we are able to go only to a certain depth at a time. Some of our pain is so intense that we must deal with it in degrees. We are ready to face only so much at a time. Then it may be awhile before we are ready to deal with more. Forgiveness is to choose as an act of our will to release whatever it is. We must continue to forgive because that is how we eventually truly break free. As an example of something you might have to forgive more than once, there was a situation that recently occurred.

> *(Jamie)* My husband and I were on a road trip to the Atlanta airport with our pastor en route to Kenya. The three of us were conversing about the reason why we had changed pediatricians. The one we had started out with did not keep good records. I shared the sordid tale with our pastor. The story goes like this. I had taken our baby girl to the doctor for her checkup and shots. Normally, she would have received two shots, but because they had run

out of one of the shot serums, she had only received one. We were to get her back for the other makeup shot. I normally took the kids to the doctor myself, but this particular time I was unable to, so Alan was going to do that for me. I had reminded him the night before and also again that next morning of her just needing one shot because I felt it was a serious notation for him to make. Acknowledging my comment, I felt he understood its importance. However, that next evening when he came home, from inside of the house I could hear Hayden crying hysterically. Walking outside to greet them, I asked what was wrong. He laughed and told me that she didn't like getting those shots (plural).

When I asked him if she'd received two shots, he confirmed she had. I immediately ran to phone the doctor to see if there could be any physical repercussions from her getting these shots back to back. Of course, they told me she would be fine. But I still wondered if they were telling me the truth. I was angry with the nurse for not checking the records but even more mad at Alan because he had acted as if he was listening to me, while in reality he had not. Why had I even bothered?

Unknown to him, it was a hot button for me. As a child, I had grown up in a home with four kids. In order to maintain sanity, my mother would tune us out while we were talking to her. It made me feel she didn't think I had anything important to say. It was hurtful to me that Alan had not listened to something I deemed as important. I think I would have felt better if he had acknowledged his part in the mishap and been sensitive to the potential danger of it.

Instead, he acted as if it was no big deal since she was going to be all right. He said he figured that since the nurse had the records right there that she knew better than I did what Hayden needed. His nonchalant attitude made me angrier along with the fact that it had never been appropriately resolved. On our way to Atlanta that day, hostility was building in me the further my story progressed.

As I finished my story, I realized I had gotten worked up in my delivery. As I looked at our pastor, I could see by his expression that I was *way* more stirred up than need be. After a moment he responded, "Well Jamie, it seems you are still dealing with some unresolved anger on this one." He was half kidding and half not! I was so embarrassed. By the way, after Alan read this chapter and realized that he'd never apologized to me about this, he did. There was total restoration in that scenario of hurt for me.

Not only do we need to learn to forgive others, but we also need to learn to forgive ourselves. Some people have a harder time forgiving themselves. "If we haven't forgiven ourselves of something, how can we forgive others?" (Delores Huerta). Romans 3:23-25 (NLT) says,

For all have sinned; all fall short of God's glorious standard. Yet now God in His gracious kindness declares us not guilty. He has done this through Christ Jesus, who has freed us by taking away our sins. For God sent Jesus to take the punishment for our sins and to satisfy God's anger against us. We are made right with God when we believe that Jesus shed his blood, sacrificing his life for us.

(Jamie) I am still required to take thoughts captive. I

> sometimes wonder, *What if I'd done that differently?* We just can't allow ourselves to submit to that attituude of "regret." That is the work of the enemy. This is why we have a Redeemer. Jesus redeems everything. How about that! He covers over our mistakes and makes it right. We are redeemed. Yes! As a parent, I used to find myself looking back on ways I'd responded with my children and wishing I had said or done some things differently. But Jesus is there to be my Redeemer, as a parent or whatever situation I find myself regretting. Finally, I reached a point where I said, NO MORE REGRET. Regret is not from God. It is torment, which comes from the tormentor.

We have a Redeemer, and He covers our mistakes. He knows we are doing the best we can. That doesn't mean that we are excused from making an apology when needed. It means that if we make a mistake, we take responsibility for our part, asking forgiveness for what was done wrong. Life is too short to be looking back, having regret, and wishing something were different. Learn from the mistake. It is never too late to change.

The Holy Spirit is the Redeemer; He is the repairer of the breach. He will help us to forgive ourselves. He will help us to forgive our spouse. Unforgiveness is like a ball and chain that you drag around with you. It weighs on you. It is painful. Why would you want to keep it? Forgiveness puts wings on our burdens. "Forgiveness is the most tender part of love" (John Sheffield).

A PRAYER FOR YOUR MARRIAGE

Dear Lord,
Thank You that freely forgiving and apologizing releases us from bondage. As an act of our will, we choose to forgive those who have offended us. Thank You that the Helper shows us that forgiveness is not only for our offender(s) but is also for us. We ask You, Holy Spirit, to remind us to take hold of this revelation and apply it to our daily walk with You. Thank You, Jesus!

Chapter Thirteen

The Money Pit

(Alan) Giving is a matter of the heart. In God's economy, we receive when we give. It strengthens our faith. It is an investment for eternity. It blesses us in return and brings joy to our hearts. What we give comes back to us; it is called the principle of "sowing and reaping." This principle does not apply only to finances; it applies to any way you give of yourself—thoughts, words, or deeds.

Give, and it will be given to you: a good measure, pressed down, shaken together and running over will be put into your bosom. For with the same measure that you use, it will be measured back to you (Luke 6:38 NKJ).

The Bible contains more verses discussing finances than heaven, hell, prayer, or faith. Seventy percent of Americans live paycheck to paycheck today, and over 1.5 million people file for bankruptcy ever year. Debt is the center of the current financial crisis. It's no wonder that Jesus addressed money more than any of these other issues. God knows that where our money is, there our heart is also!

(Alan) I remember when Jamie and I were first married, and we made the commitment to give back to God. At that time, we did it based upon obligation rather than love for God. We attended a church that had a very religious approach to tithing. Since then, our motivation for giving has changed to one of love for Him and a desire to see His kingdom advance. The moment we began to honor God by giving back to Him, we began to experience a supernatural protection on our finances and every other aspect of our lives. God loves to provide for those who are generous with their resources.

There is a chain of grocery stores in our home town of Birmingham founded by the Bruno family. When they first started out as a corner grocery downtown, Joe Bruno and his wife were generous and compassionate. Those less fortunate would be provided a hot meal in the Bruno home. The Brunos were a very savvy business family, but the real secret of their success was their generosity.

Proverbs 3:9-10 (NAS) says, *"Honor the Lord from your wealth, And from the first of all your produce; So your barns will be filled with plenty, And your vats will overflow with new wine."* We are convinced that we should give a tithe to God first before paying bills or saving. A tithe in biblical terms simply means ten percent. It is an act of worship to place Him first in priority.

Our giving to Him is a reflection of our dependence and reliance upon Him as our source of blessing. We give because He first gave to us.

Whoever can be trusted with very little can also be trusted with much, and whoever is dishonest with very little will also be dishonest with much. So if you have not been trustworthy in

> *handling worldly wealth, who will trust you with true riches?* (Luke 16:10-11 NIV).

John 3: 16 (ESV) says, "*For God so loved the world that He gave his only son . . .*" God is a giver—the ultimate giver. He gave the greatest and most perfect gift of His Son to us. Jesus came to be the sacrificial Lamb for those of us who acknowledge Him.

Everything belongs to God anyway. If God is the Creator of everything, then everything is His. We belong to Him, and our talents, abilities, and our "stuff" belong to Him also. Our money is His. So why don't we give what is His to Him by tithing? The Bible speaks of tithing saying,

> *Stop loving this evil world and all that it offers you, for when you love these things you show that you really do not love God; for all these worldly things, these evil desires . . . the ambition to buy everything that appeals to you, and the pride that comes from wealth and importance—these are not from God. They are from this evil world itself* (1 John 2:15 TLB).

Every married couple desperately needs to have a financial plan and agree on how they will spend their money. Money problems are a primary source of conflict and strife among married couples. We have counseled countless couples having financial difficulties, and it always seems to come back to a lack of agreement concerning finances. Proverbs 21:5 (NIV) says, "*The plans of the diligent lead to profit as surely as haste leads to poverty.*" *We* need to be intentional with our finances and make responsible purchases, buying only what we can afford within our budget. There are many excellent tools available to assist us in living within a budget.

Two of the best resources we've found are Dave Ramsey's study, *Financial Peace University* and Larry Burkett's *Crown Ministries.* Both will show how to get out of debt, stay out of debt, and guide you in wise financial decision making. "*It is for freedom that Christ has set us free. Stand firm, then, and do not let yourselves be burdened again by a yoke of (financial) slavery*" (Galatians 5:1 NIV). "*The borrower is servant to the lender*" (Proverbs 22:7 NIV).

(Alan) Our early years were difficult financially. I would go out and purchase items such as a new watch (I'm a watch nut) or a suit without discussing it with Jamie. Believe me, it was the source of much conflict back then. We finally came to understand that we had to agree before making major purchases.

We've been married now for twenty-four years, and I must confess that for twenty-one of those years we had no written budget. I had some rough idea in my head of what we were spending. We always spent more than I thought we did. The one thing we had going for us was that we were givers, and God was gracious to us through those years. We now live by a written budget. Our finances are better than they have ever been, and it is incredibly freeing to know they are in order. I encourage you to seek the Holy Spirit as you make plans and create a budget that works for your lifestyle. God desires to bless us when we honor His words concerning money. He desires for us to join Him in advancing His kingdom!

Malachi 3:10 (NAS) says,

"Bring the whole tithe into the storehouse, so that there may be food in My house, and test Me now in this," says the Lord of hosts, "if I will not open for you the windows of heaven, and pour out for you a blessing until it overflows."

(Jamie) My dad was a very conscientious provider for our

family. Because of my mother's health condition, she was not able to work to retirement. My dad felt added pressure due to my mother's unfortunate situation. Because all four of the kids were two years apart from one another, there was a time when all four of us were in college at the same time (my oldest sister started on her master's right after college).

My dad had always said that, as our parent, he felt it was his responsibility to put us through college. He tells me that for the longest time he would go back and try to figure out mathematically just how he was able to do it. He would say, "It just didn't add up to be enough, yet I was able to do it." It was no mystery to me; I know that because my dad was always a generous tither, God honored him by multiplying his finances. Our God is generous and gracious.

Both of our parents provided for us well and are very generous, while at the same time they are good stewards with the finances with which God has blessed them. They have modeled the importance of giving to the kingdom. So, both of us grew up with a good biblical example. But there are some of us who may not have had that kind of model. The good news is that through the power of the Holy Spirit, wisdom is available for us to manage our finances well. He is a great teacher and is waiting to help. All that we need to do is simply ask Him. We encourage you to establish these principles in your home now. It is never too late.

A PRAYER FOR YOUR MARRIAGE

Dear Lord,
Thank You for the blessing of giving. You gave the greatest gift of all when You sent your Son, Jesus. He took all of the sin, disease, sickness, pain, and poverty upon Himself so that He would be our sacrificial Lamb. Because You have given so much to us, we want to give back to You our tithe, and indeed our lives. Make us mindful of the importance of agreement in financial decision making. And because we are generous with You, we are able to manage our finances in a manner that pleases You. Thank You that Your Holy Spirit is the best financial advisor or consultant we could have. Thank You that You desire prosperity for us in every way. We invite the Holy Spirit, our financial guide, to lead us into Your perfect plan for our finances.

Chapter Fourteen

Suitable Helper

(Jamie) We once counseled some newlyweds who were both older when they married. The wife, having never been married before, wanted to know what a normal marriage was and how it worked. Much to her dissatisfaction, I told her that there was no such thing as a "normal" marriage. Every marriage has partners with unique backgrounds, circumstances, and preferences. Therefore, their marriage would also be unique. Wanting a more definitive answer, she told me that neither of their parents had good marriages and that she needed a model to follow so her marriage could have a better start. She wanted to be a suitable helper for him and vice versa.

The best thing to give your enemy is forgiveness; to a friend your heart; to a child a good example; to a father, honor; to your mother, conduct that will make her proud of you; to yourself, respect; to all people, charity (Arthur Balfour).

We are taking liberty with Balfour's quote for our purposes. Maybe it should read, "The best thing to give your

> spouse is forgiveness; to your spouse, your heart; to them, a good example; to them, honor; conduct that will make them proud of you; respect and charity."

Marriage was God's idea; it is a very good one indeed, initiated through His creation of Adam and Eve. The Bible is the best resource for discovering how we can be a "suitable helper." Referring to the Holy Spirit, Jesus said, *"And I will ask the Father, and He will give you another Comforter (Counselor, Helper, Intercessor, Advocate, Strengthener, and Standby) that He may remain with you forever"* (John 14:16 AMP). The Greek word *parakletos*, translated as "helper," literally means, "one who is called beside." Just as Jesus sent the Holy Spirit as our spiritual helper, so a spouse is "called beside" to be a "helper" in our marriage.

In our walk as Christians, we invite the Holy Spirit into our lives. We consult with the Holy Spirit for decision making, guidance, and direction. We trust the Holy Spirit as a facet of God who knows and wants His best for us. *"If you then, being evil, know how to give good gifts to your children, how much more shall your heavenly Father give the Holy Spirit to those who ask Him"* (Luke 11:13 Ryrie Study Bible).

The Holy Spirit is the third Person of the Trinity, the mediator, and the intercessor within the believer to reveal God's will. As the Helper, the Holy Spirit will guide (Acts 8:29 NIV), give assurance (Romans 8:26 NIV), be teacher to (1 John 2:27 NIV), intercede (Romans 8:26 NIV), comfort (John 14:16 NIV), sanctify (2 Thessalonians 2:13 NIV), accomplish regeneration (John 3:16 NIV), make you aware of sin (John 16:8 NIV), convince you of the truth of the Gospel (John 16:8 NIV), encourage you to witness (Acts 1:8 NIV), help destroy the power of sin in your life (Romans 8: 2-6 NIV), and lead and counsel (Romans 8:14 NIV).

Although we are not saying that you are to be your spouse's Holy Spirit, there is a similarity between the role of the Holy Spirit and the role of a marriage partner. Quite often, the Holy Spirit will speak through one spouse for the other person's benefit. As Christians, intimacy with our spouse should relationally mirror the type of spiritual intimacy, accountability, and vulnerability that we experience with God. Our spouse is called to work beside us throughout life to provide physical, spiritual, and emotional support. And just as the Holy Spirit is our teacher, so can our spouse be one from whom we learn. The different perspectives a husband and wife bring into a situation can provide a healthy balance. Our spouse should be our counterpart that completes us. "Two are better than one because they have a good return for their labor" (Ecclesiastes 4:9).

> *(Jamie)* There is a story that I share with women who don't like the way their husbands are treating them. It is a story of a woman named Polly who lived in the early 1900s. She was married to a man named Smith Wigglesworth. At the time, Smith was a backslidden Christian, but he later became one of the greatest healing evangelists of all time. He was so consumed with his plumbing business that he became resentful of his wife's time spent at church meetings.
>
> One night he told her not to go to church. But she had always gone to church on Wednesday night. She knew that he was testing her faithfulness to God, so she went as usual. When she returned home, the front door was locked. She went to the back of the house and came in that way. They had a good laugh over it. She demonstrates a perfect picture of unconditional love because she had every right to be angry, but she chose to accept him and find humor in the situation instead.

God brought a woman like Polly into Smith's life because He knew the type of woman that would draw out the best in him despite his gruff exterior. She saw him with spiritual (eternal) eyes. In other words, she was able to draw out his potential. Smith Wigglesworth was gifted in a ministry that witnessed miraculous healing and restoration, physically, mentally, spiritually, and emotionally during his lifetime. See the book, *Smith Wigglesworth--The Complete Collection of His Life Teachings* for more on his ministry.

Polly chose not to focus on those areas that were an aggravation but instead knew there was good in her husband. As his counterpart, she was exactly what he needed. Polly knew the biblical truth of calling forth things that are not as though they were, as in Romans 4:17. She was a suitable helper for Smith!

Our intimacy with the Holy Spirit should occur in a state of trust and total vulnerability. Couples should share this same trusted intimacy. Husbands and wives should be able to show weakness and vulnerability without the fear of judgment, rejection, or retaliation from their spouse.

In a healthy marriage, the relationship is based on trust. The spouse is a trustworthy confidante. For example, we would not want our spouse to talk to a friend or family member about our shortcomings or intimate problems, so we wouldn't do that to them either. Partners should feel safe and protected with each other. Perhaps as in Balfour's quote, the best thing we can give our spouse is love.

You've seen a three-legged race where two people each have a leg tied together, and they race toward the finish line. They must communicate and coordinate their movements in order to win the race. It's the same challenge in marriage as we learn how to function in harmony, becoming suitable helpers through the power of the Holy Spirit as our standby.

A PRAYER FOR YOUR MARRIAGE

Dear Lord,
Help us to become better acquainted with Your Word as it helps us to have a better relationship. Help us to be mindful of ways the Holy Spirit can assist in our marriage as "one who is called beside." Help us to trust the leading of the Holy Spirit in our lives. Thank You for the different ways You use (spouse's name) as an earthly helper and the Holy Spirit as a heavenly helper. Thank You that You want us to understand better our role as suitable helpers. Help us to develop a trust and intimacy with You so that we will become one in spirit.

Chapter Fifteen

Collision

(Jamie) Alan was an accountant for a large company when we met. I was a graphic designer for the same company. Alan called himself a "bean counter" and I was supposedly the "temperamental artist," both stereotypes that are associated with these professions. Truly, neither of us fit our typecast roles. Alan has quite the eye for style and design while I am pretty even-tempered. Alan eventually got out of accounting and is totally happy in sales as an insurance broker. I came home after fifteen years in the corporate world. We had two young children when God called me to be an "at-home" mom.

Alan brings good business sense, practicality, and stability to our marriage, whereas I like being spontaneous and enjoy creative pursuits. For two people with such different professions, I have been amazed at how common our likes are in other ways. We both loved our first little house. We pooled our furniture, and it came together quite well. We were in agreement about decorating decisions and enjoyed the same types of food, interests, etc.

I'd heard horror stories of couples not being able to agree even on everyday dishes. You can imagine what decorating a house could be like for a couple like this, or, worse yet, picking out a house. This would be just a preview of coming attractions. For anyone not married who is reading this book, relax. There is a meshing process that takes place where each individual's tastes blend together with the others into the couple's own unique style. Then there are those couples where one person doesn't care to have any input and the other selects everything. I am glad Alan wants input. It feels more like "ours" because he does.

"There are a few rules I know to be true about love and marriage. If you don't *respect* the other person, you're gonna have a lot of trouble. If you don't *compromise*, you're gonna have a lot of trouble. If you can't *talk openly* about what goes on between you, you're gonna have a lot of trouble. And if you don't have a *common set of values* in life, you're gonna have a lot of trouble. Your values must be alike. And the biggest one of those values . . . Your belief in the *importance* of marriage" (From the book, *Tuesdays with Morrie* by Mitch Albom, about a mentoring relationship of life lessons between a professor and a former student).

Do you remember the commercial where someone is walking along eating a chocolate bar, and another person approaches from the other direction eating peanut butter? Because neither one of them is paying attention to where they are going, they end up running into one another. One says, "Hey, you got chocolate in my peanut butter," and the other responds, "You got peanut butter in my chocolate!" Hence the Reese's peanut butter cup was born. As they both taste this creation, with a grin of approval, a marketing campaign is waged.

Well, that is how a good marriage should work. We don't just get peanut butter anymore; we have a win-win and get a Reese's instead. When Jamie and I married, I had never even tasted olives or tabouli, now they are just about my favorite foods. Likewise, Jamie had never liked Brussels sprouts or tasted crème brulee; now they are regulars in our diet. Our tastes have been blended together to become something different. Part of that oneness we have talked about carries over into every part of our lives (i.e., books we read, trips we take, movies we see, etc.).

In marriage there are combined efforts for a good return. Initially we are not quick to see the benefit. Instead, we see that it is not "the way I used to do it when it was just me" or "I have never done it that way before." But each member of a couple brings differences that, when combined, create something new and better. In effect, we become a different person from who we once were when we share our lives with each other.

Marriage is a coming together of two different family cultures to form a new one. Sometimes it is a collision rather than a smooth transition. That is why respect for each other's differences is so important. Sometimes we can be repulsed by the different ways our spouse does things.

When Jamie and I married, it was a very smooth transition in most ways. However, in the kitchen, Jamie did things differently. She liked to cook and make a mess with a huge pile of dishes in the sink. My method was to wash the dirty dishes as we cooked. She drove me crazy, and I drove her crazy with my neat nick style. We had to compromise and meet in the middle. Now we cook and then wash the dishes later.

> *(Jamie)* We have both evolved over the years. We just celebrated our twenty-fourth wedding anniversary. Alan has so many wonderful qualities. He has always been very motivated. When we married, he went back to school to get his

master's degree. Then he later got certified. He's quite courageous. An unexpected corporate decision allowed him to change careers after being an accountant for ten years. Establishing himself in a new profession took patience and perseverance. The great thing about what he is doing now is that the knowledge from his past experiences in accounting, from his MBA and CPA, were preparatory tools for what he does so well now.

What we perceived as a difficult time in Alan's career path turned out to be just what God wanted to happen to get Alan to where he ultimately needed to be. I know that we were led every step of the way. It was an oddly laid out path to follow, which with our natural eye would not have been what we would have wanted but was exactly right.

We're slowly getting to where we aren't second-guessing God anymore. It is wonderful to be married to a man who loves his job! It makes all of the difference. There was a lot of intense prayer going on during that time for us, though. It wasn't always easy. I remember when we first got married, Alan was not as verbal as I was. He was also unhappy at work, and therefore there were angry outbursts toward me that I did not understand.

We really had to talk through a lot of this baggage. Fortunately for me, Alan realized and cared how unhappy it was making me. He worked hard to break through the anger issues and to let me know where he was mentally so that I could understand him better. It was a good time for developing improved communication.

Good communication between husbands and wives is an art form developed over time. Feedback is the key to understanding each other. We have to make sure that what we heard was actually what was said. We may misinterpret what was said and read something into it that was not intended. So many things can get in the way of our communication: we had a bad day at work or home, we are tired, angry, etc. The enemy loves to get in the way and cause a misunderstanding and wreak havoc.

As we grew as Christians and in our relationship with God, our marriage relationship got better. If you are both working on your relationship with God, everything will be better because you are aligning yourself with God's Word. The Holy Spirit needs to be part of the equation. As we invited the Holy Spirit into our marriage to strengthen and guide us, we began to trust Him. We learned respect for each other through the Holy Spirit's guidance. We learned to compromise and create our own way of doing things, and we learned how to communicate with each other. The Holy Spirit was and is a great teacher. We had to learn to let go and let God, being led by the Spirit.

A PRAYER FOR YOUR MARRIAGE

Dear Lord,

Help us to see the benefit in our differences as we learn the art of compromise in our marriage. Holy Spirit, help us learn to respect our spouse, to negotiate our values for shared values, to talk openly with each other, and to put You first in our relationship. We ask You to bless our combined efforts with a good return as we become one.

Chapter Sixteen

"A" for Attitude

(Jamie) I remember one day walking up to a counter in the city courthouse to pay for a license. The girl behind the counter began chewing me out. I couldn't figure out the source of her anger towards me. Stunned, I stepped out of her line and went into another. The girl next to her said, "That is not the same girl that gave you a hard time a minute ago" and my clerk retorted, "Yes it is. She is wearing that purple sweater." I made an unfortunate purple selection that morning in my dressing closet. I didn't know what had transpired before, but obviously a young lady in purple with a bad attitude had an encounter with this woman just prior to my being there.

I remember feeling horrified, having everyone stare at me as if I had done something terribly wrong. I wanted to say, "I've never seen this woman before in my life!" Anyway, she had encountered a bad attitude in purple, and she in turn spewed her bad attitude on an unsuspecting me. Later, I marveled at the gumption of this public servant's behavior toward the public and wondered why I hadn't reported her.

We must make a choice. My father had a short fuse during my growing up years. Now I understand that the stress of supporting a large family was the source, but it had so unnerved me as a child that I had determined not to marry a man with that same quality.

Well, guess what happened after we were married. That's right. I'll never forget my first exposure to an angry outburst in our new home. We were painting our home's exterior together along with Alan's dad. Alan was painting the front door with a thick oil paint, and it was becoming a streaking, mucky mess. I was rendered speechless as I watched my husband throw a temper tantrum in front of us. I couldn't believe what I was witnessing. I had thought this man didn't have an "ill-tempered" bone in his body. In retaliation to my husband's tempers, I would get mad. You can imagine what a lovely combination that was. Neither one of us was being productive in either case. We both needed an attitude change. Thankfully, we eventually worked through those issues.

"The longer I live, the more I realize the impact of attitude on life. Attitude, to me, is more important than facts. It is more important than the past, than education, than failures, than successes, than what people think or say or do. It is more important than appearance, giftedness, or skill. It will make or break a company . . . a church . . . a home . . . a marriage. The remarkable thing is we have a choice everyday regarding the attitude we embrace for that day. We cannot change the fact that people will act a certain way. We cannot change the inevitable. The only thing we can do is play on the string we have, and that is our attitude. I am convinced that life is ten percent of what happens to me, and ninety percent how I react to it. And so it is with you . . . we are in charge of our attitudes" (Charles Swindoll).

Attitude is what we make of it. Have you ever been around someone where you can almost see a rain cloud over that person's head? We don't want to get wet too, do we? We can't get away from them fast enough, can we? Some people don't even realize it about themselves. Many people like this were brought up in homes where a parent had this attitude. I have a friend who said that her mother was one of these types of people, but her father was delightful. She said one day when she was old enough to see the contrast, she said to herself, *I choose to be like him*. We have to one day make the choice of how we choose to be. Our attitudes in large part make us who we are.

Thankfulness is one of those attitudes that is lacking in today's society. Cicero said, "A thankful heart is not only the greatest virtue, but the parent of all other virtues." Scripture says we are to give thanks with a grateful heart, no matter what the circumstances (1 Thessalonians 5:18 AMP). Thankfulness is the key to contentedness. If we are thankful, then we look for things to be thankful for instead of things about which we complain.

We have all experienced disappointments and for some even tragedy. As Chuck Swindoll pointed out, it is ninety percent how we react to the things that happen to us and only ten percent the event itself. Scripture is a wonderful source of comfort and strength when situations go haywire. It helps us focus on the proper attitude. *"Now may the God of all hope fill you with all joy and peace in believing, that you may abound in hope by the power of the Holy Spirit"* (Romans 15:13 NKJ).

The Holy Spirit is the key to unlocking the power of God's promise of joy and peace in our lives. As we focus on the person of the Holy Spirit and God's promises, our problems fade away into the background. Our worries can simply disappear because we have one who loves us that is greater than all our problems and worries. What good is it to worry anyway? As Scripture says, who can add a day to their life through worry? And whatever things are true, honorable, right, pure, lovely, of good repute, of excellence or praiseworthy, let your mind dwell on these things.

(Alan) Early in our marriage, I had a very negative thing happen to me in my career. The company that I worked for at the time decided to eliminate my position. I went into work one morning, had a meeting with my boss just before lunch, and by lunchtime, I was out on the street without a job.

I remember calling Jamie telling her that I would not be at work the rest of the day or any other day. Jamie met me at home, and we both had a good cry together. Then we both went outside into our backyard and sat down to pray and contemplate our future. It was at that time I decided to change careers. I really did not enjoy accounting work and had desired to make a change into a sales career but had not acted on it out of fear. We both decided to look at my job loss as an opportunity to at last do what I had always wanted to do. Jamie was wonderfully supportive and backed me 100 percent as I made the change to sales.

I remember being excited about the career change. It was hard at first, but we both felt it was the right decision. It was one of the first times that we stepped out in faith and believed God's Word. God did bless us in every way. Up until that time, we both worked, and I really could not imagine a situation in which I could support us and allow Jamie to come home and be with our children.

It was several years after my career change when we decided that Jamie would quit her job and come home. After another year or so, I had been able to replace all the income she made while working. We both are convinced that God honored our positive attitude during those years and blessed us because of it.

Dr. David Viscott gave a teaching called "Mastering Your Feelings." Basically, the message is that we should not permit another person to affect our mood. In that event, we are giving them the power or permission to control us and our moods when only we need to be the one in control of that in our lives. That is why one of the fruits of the Spirit is self-control. Maintaining self-control is another way that we set ourselves apart from the world. *"A person without self-control is as defenseless as a city with broken-down walls"* (Proverbs 25:28 NLT).

Inviting the Holy Spirit to guide us in response to difficult people and situations releases power for a godly response. Our attitude is key in facilitating the movement of the Spirit and in unlocking the power of God's promises of joy and peace in our lives. We have one who loves us that is greater than all our problems and worries.

A PRAYER FOR YOUR MARRIAGE

Dear Lord,
Please help make us mindful of our attitude. "Create in us a clean heart, O God, and renew a right, persevering, and steadfast spirit within us" (Psalms 51:10 AMP). It is our desire to honor You in thought, word, and deed. By the power of the Holy Spirit, help us to respond with self-control no matter how extreme we find our situations to be. "Restore to me the joy of Your salvation and uphold me with a willing spirit" (Psalm 51:12 AMP).

Chapter Seventeen

Humble Pie

(Alan) Maybe it's a guy thing. I mean the problem we seem to have with humility. Why is it so-o-o difficult to say, "I'm sorry"? Jamie and I have never argued much, but when we do, it is usually me that needs to confess and say that I was wrong. I used to feel like the Fonz on Happy Days. My mouth would get stuck saying, "I'm sorry."

Humility was difficult for me until the Holy Spirit was able to get through and help me understand that my lack of humility was simply pride. I did not want to admit that I had been wrong, and then my pride would kick in and I would try to justify my actions. I always wanted to prove that I was right. Big mistake! It is much easier now to just admit when I am wrong and go on with life. No big deal.

Pride is concerned with *who* is right. Humility is concerned with *what* is right. —Ezra Taft Benson

Have you ever heard anyone say, "This humble pie sure tastes good"? The word *humility* is one word with which we don't like to be associated. We think it is a sign of weakness. We don't like it because we really don't understand it. It is defined in *Webster's Dictionary* as "having or showing consciousness of one's shortcomings; not proud." We don't like the word because we don't like to admit that we make mistakes, have shortcomings, or because we don't want people to know what those shortcomings are. Why? Because we believe that others will think less of us. We already know that no one is perfect, so what does it matter to admit to a mistake or shortcoming?

Another definition of *humble* is "low in condition, rank, and position." This is another reason why we don't like to be connected with this word. Isn't it interesting that God calls Christians to be humble, yet we resist and don't want to obey that particular command. Maybe the reason we don't understand humility is because Scripture defines it differently from the world. The Bible says, *"Humble yourself in the sight of the Lord and He will lift you up"* (James 4:10 NKJ).

Many of us think that humility is allowing someone to walk all over us. Let us clarify true humility. Jesus brought about the recognition of His humility by demonstrating His absolute dependence on His Father. Jesus said, *"I do nothing of Myself; but as My Father taught Me, I speak these things"* (John 8:28 NKJ). That kind of "doing" can only be done if you REALLY know the Father so well that you know how He would respond.

For example, Jesus was described as humble, but do you remember the incident with the money changers in the temple (John 2:13-15 NKJ) where He overturned tables and told them to leave? Does this sound like the behavior of a humble person? Not according to Webster's definition. Jesus was exhibiting righteous anger. He was responding as the Father would have responded had He been in that situation.

The money changers had become opportunists. They were taking advantage of the pilgrims who had traveled to Jerusalem for Passover. They did not have their own sacrificial animals with them. They had no other choice than to purchase the animals that were available there for a sacrifice. The money changers were making it into a highly profitable business, turning the outer courts of the temple into a noisy circus of activity.

Jesus was unconcerned about His own well-being or how people viewed Him. His concern was for His Father. The disrespect shown towards His Father's house caused righteous anger to rise up within Him.

God understands our human nature, so why do you think He asks us to do something He knows we don't want to do? He is showing us a better way. Humility is a powerful act. Have you ever had someone come to you fully confessing that what he or she had done was wrong? It is so freeing for you and for that person. You can release it and move on, and that person can too. It is awful when someone starts giving you reasons and excuses or, worse yet, blaming someone else for why something happened rather than saying, "I'm sorry. I messed up! Will you forgive me?"

There are good friends and relatives who throw away a relationship because of being unable to admit to a mistake. Unfortunately, this happens in marriages all the time. Humility keeps us from being proud. If we are proud, we are never wrong. What happens in a marriage relationship when two proud people are never wrong? They damage the relationship by being unwilling to compromise. It is better to "die to self." There can be no resolution when neither party takes any of the blame.

> *(Jamie)* I had an altercation with a maid who worked for me. She got mad at me and told me that she was leaving her job. The next day she called and apologized. I remember being surprised by her confession and having more respect for her because of it. It takes a big person to do that. It takes a person who is secure in their identity in Christ, one who is not concerned about what man thinks

> but with what God thinks, one who wants to make a situation right. This is the connection with Jesus in the Temple. He was offended because His Father was offended. He was only concerned with what His Father thought. We should respond with this kind of humility.

There is a difference between a peacemaker and a peacekeeper. *"Blessed are the peacemakers, for they shall be called the sons of God"* (Matthew 5:9 NKJ). Peacemakers operate in a just and peaceful manner. Peacekeepers keep the peace at all cost. Peace becomes more important than anything else becomes and causes the person to excuse wrong or sin just to keep peace. This is not being a peacemaker; it is a character weakness. Avoidance of potentially unpleasant people or situations is cowardly.

Boundaries, by Henry Cloud, is a good book for learning about healthy boundaries in relationships. There are times in our lives where we need to know when to say no. It is all right to say no. This can be a huge source of conflict in a marriage relationship. Many people have difficulty saying no, but this response is healthy. Some people get so burdened because of their inability to say no that it leads to added stress and affects their health. If you don't know what healthy boundaries are, don't feel bad; most people could use some help in this area.

> *(Alan)* I have a friend who was about to get married to a lovely girl. In planning the wedding, he had discovered that his future sister-in-law wanted to have a shower for them and do everything, including making the guest list, without input from them (the couple getting married). My friend was shocked that the sister-in-law proposed this without any opposition. His fiancé said that her sister had been like this all of her life. Whose fault is that? *Why had this been going on for so long?* he wondered. No one had

said, NO to her. This could make him a very unpopular guy with his new wife's sister. This illustrates a boundary violation.

Clothe yourselves with humility toward one another, for God is opposed to the proud but gives grace to the humble. Humble yourselves therefore under the mighty hand of God that He may exalt you at the proper time, casting all your anxiety upon Him, because He cares for you (1 Peter 5:5-7 RSB).

Are you willing to let go and let God do for you what these verses promise? If we will yield to the leading of the Holy Spirit, He promises to show us a better way. As Third Cord, He is our counselor and advocate in *all* things. It is good to add this humble delicacy to your marriage diet . . . humble pie a la mode. Bon appétit!

A PRAYER FOR YOUR MARRIAGE

Dear Lord,
Thank You for this excellent virtue of humility that You desire for us to practice. Help us to willingly operate in humility and understand its true meaning in our marriage. We invite the Holy Spirit to teach us how to walk humbly with others. Reveal to us when our flesh resists Your leading. Help us to be more concerned with what You think than what man thinks. Help us to pursue sincere reconciliation, spoken not just from our mouth but also from our heart. Help us to be peacemakers rather than peacekeepers. Thank you that the Holy Spirit leads us in finding healthy boundaries. Finally, help us to be clothed with humility towards one another.

Chapter Eighteen

Avoiding Pitfalls

(Jamie) We have known a couple for several years now where the husband is walking a fine line between family man and dabbling in the gay lifestyle. He wants to have his wife and family on one hand and satisfy his sexual curiosity on the other. It started years ago with the husband's addiction to pornography and slowly evolved from looking at pornography to acting out his fantasies. It appears that he has finally made a choice to commit to his family and leave his alternate lifestyle behind.

Galatians 5:16-17 (TLB) says,

I advise you to obey the Holy Spirit's instruction. He will tell you where to go and what to do, and then you won't be doing all the wrong things your evil nature wants to do. For we naturally love to do evil things that are just the opposite of the thing the Holy Spirit wants us to do; and the good things we want to do when the Spirit has His way with us are just the opposite of our natural desires. These two forces within us are constantly fighting each other to win control over us, and our wishes are never free from pressures.

We are living in a very self-centered, self-gratifying society. We see and hear ads that promote "having it your way," "If it feels good, do it," and "You deserve it." All of these endorse selfish pleasure. Sexuality is blatantly used and accepted today as a strategy for advertising. No wonder our society is seeing more sex-related criminal acts as well as more addiction to pornography and sex than ever before. It is repeatedly in our faces through multimedia sources.

The Holy Spirit has great wisdom and instruction for us. Our role is to ask Him to direct us in it. He will tell us where to go and what to do if we will only allow Him. He is the Third Cord of the three-fold cord. He is a Friend who will walk alongside to warn, protect, and assist us. Wouldn't you want a friend like that?

We get wisdom from the Holy Spirit when our spirits (hearts) are joined with His. We must acknowledge our sin nature and be willing to submit our spirit to the Holy Spirit. Most people know when they are doing wrong; they have just made a choice to override their conscience and submit to their sinful natures.

Our weaknesses provide a crack in the door for Satan to come in and influence us. We must be aware of Satan's schemes and shut the door, not allowing him entry. There is a constant battle taking place within our minds between good and evil, right and wrong, life and death choices. To make right choices we need to keep our focus on God and the things above, which includes prayer, reading our Bible, and fellowship with other believers. What we think about we eventually become.

We will have to battle our sin nature all of our lives. We all have areas where we are weak and need help. The Holy Spirit is there at the right time when we need Him to strengthen or direct us when we are tired in the battle. "You may have to fight a battle more than once to win it" (Margaret Thatcher).

If we are battling something that we don't want others to know about, perhaps we need a trusted accountability partner to run alongside us. We all need to listen to godly wisdom from people we trust. Inquire of the Holy Spirit.

(Jamie) I have a dear friend who had been divorced from her first husband. As she entered into the dating scene, she met someone with whom she was very attracted. There were major differences in their lives that I thought would make them incompatible. Because of my genuine love and concern for my friend's future, and at the risk of losing her friendship, I expressed my concerns. Fortunately for me, my friend listened. She is currently married to her perfect match. She waited for God's best for her!

(Alan) I meet with an accountability partner several times a month. Jamie and I have always prayed together and given each other the right to speak into the other's life. But Ken and I get together Saturday mornings at a local Starbucks to talk and pray. Over a period of several years, we have become quite transparent with one another. Sharing the struggles and temptations we are experiencing has been wonderful. We are able to give each other godly wisdom from an objective viewpoint.

It is great to know that I have another man praying for me who knows my weaknesses and loves me unconditionally. Jamie has an accountability partner with whom she prays weekly. Together they have prayed our families through many tough situations. There is such power in agreement when two believers pray together.

God sent His Holy Spirit to convict our hearts when we do wrong. We must choose either the path of righteousness or destruction. He desires us to choose well. Psalms 16:7-11 (NKJ) says,

I will bless the Lord who has given me counsel; My heart also instructs me in the night seasons, I have set the Lord always before me; Because he is at my right hand I shall not be moved. Therefore my heart is glad, and my glory rejoices; My flesh also will rest in hope. For You will not leave my soul in Sheol, Nor will You allow Your Holy One to see corruption. You will show me the path of life; In Your presence is fullness of joy; At Your right hand are pleasures forevermore.

God wants to see us protected from the pitfalls in this world. He wants us to live pure and holy lives. The Helper is there for us; He will tell us where to go and what to do. If you ask Him, He will show you the way! *"This is the way, walk ye in it"* (Isaiah 30:21 NKJ).

A PRAYER FOR YOUR MARRIAGE

Dear Lord,
Thank You for the life-giving conviction of the Holy Spirit. We know that it is there to protect us. We invite the Holy Spirit into our marriage in order to avoid the pitfalls of this world. You don't condemn but desire abundant life for us. Holy Spirit show us Your way!

Chapter Nineteen

Back on Track

(Alan and Jamie) It makes us smile to hear of successful marriages that last over decades. We read a story in our local *Birmingham News* that featured a couple, Lecil and Marjorie Naramore, who have been married for seventy-seven years. She is ninety-three, and he is ninety-eight years old. In the article, they tell of their meeting, courtship, and marriage just as though it were yesterday. He shared the secret of their success simply by saying, "She's good to me, and I try to be good to her." The title of the article was, "All I Know Is She's Perfect."

"It's the little things that make the difference—taking 20 minutes talking to each other when the children go to bed, opening doors for one another, getting one another a cup of coffee—that lead to success in marriage," says Elizabeth Schmitz, who co-wrote *Golden Anniversaries: The Seven Secrets of Successful Marriage* with her husband, Charles. We have read about powerful examples of the Holy Spirit acting as an advocate to recreate, restore, and enrich marriages. We have also learned how we can invite the Holy Spirit into our own personal lives and into our marriage.

The Holy Spirit is the Third Cord, which binds a marriage together into a lifetime commitment honoring God's Word. If we honor God's Word, we will honor our spouse. Marriage is God's plan for man and woman to live together.

The original married couple was Adam and Eve. It was God's perfect plan to create Adam, in His image, with all the qualities and characteristics of both male and female. But God then removed Adam's female side and used it to form Eve. Adam said, "This is my flesh and my bones." The challenge in marriage is for husband and wife to be joined together again and learn to function as one.

As we understand the heart of the Father and His love for us, we are able to receive every good gift He gives. The Holy Spirit in marriage is one of those excellent gifts to be utilized and cherished. Like David, when we trust and understand God and that He has our best interests at heart, it is easy to receive His gifts and allow the Holy Spirit to direct us.

God says that we are righteous and holy, so He wants us to believe that and allow the truth of His Word to penetrate our hearts. With this understanding, we begin to act differently towards our mate. When we become whom God has said we are, it transforms us and our relationships. The Holy Spirit helps in the transformation process by reminding us of how He sees us and who He says we are.

Prayer is the single most interactive way that we communicate with our heavenly Father. There is great power when we pray in agreement as a couple. Because marriage is God's ordained and blessed way for us to live, He places great power in the relationship; and we release that power through prayer. We recommend that couples pray together regularly.

Couples who practice the art of compromise use the power of agreement to experience peace. They are able to resolve conflict working together as one. Husbands are to love their wives and wives are to respect their husbands without regard to whether they deserve it. If we will make the decision to obey His Word, then He will bless our efforts. We challenge you to acknowledge all of your spouse's good qualities and let them know that you appreciate those things about them.

God accepts us all, so we should accept our spouse as well. A quote by Carl Jung states, "We cannot change anything unless we accept it. Condemnation does not liberate, it oppresses." The first step toward change is acceptance. Once we accept ourselves (and others), we open the door to change.

Forgiveness puts wings on our burdens; it brings freedom. We can forgive our spouse because of God's forgiveness. Grace is the key that allows us to forgive our spouse and others. In a healthy marriage, couples are freely able to forgive each other. "I believe we [married couples] should always work toward these two goals: 1) overcoming our own weaknesses, 2) while allowing our spouse to have them" (Marilyn vos Savant).

Giving is an essential part of any marriage, not only giving oneself to their spouse but giving into the kingdom as well. Giving is a matter of the heart. In God's economy we receive when we give, it strengthens our faith, it is an investment for eternity, it blesses us, and in return brings joy to our hearts.

> *Give, and it shall be given to you. Good measure, pressed down, shaken together and running over, will be put into your lap. For the measure you use it will be measured back to you* (Luke 6:38 ESV).

There is nothing more exciting than seeing the hand of God move on our behalf. The more in tune we are with Him, the more we are able to be a party to His manifest power. We need to balance our knowledge of Scripture with a belief in the supernatural power of God.

Marriage was God's idea; it is a very good one indeed, initiated through His creation of Adam and Eve. The Bible is the best resource for discovering how we can be a "suitable helper." In marriage there are combined efforts for a good return. Initially we are not quick to see the benefit, but each member of a couple brings differences that, when combined, create something new and better. Our spouse is intended to be a great blessing from God to help us accomplish His will and purpose for our lives. In effect, we become a different person from who we once were when we share our lives with each other.

Good communication between husbands and wives is an art form developed over time. Feedback is the key to understanding each other. We have to let each other know that what we heard was actually what was meant. We may misinterpret what was said and read in something that was not intended. So many things can get in the way of our communication: we had a bad day at work or home, we are tired, angry, etc. The enemy loves to get in the way and cause offense or a misunderstanding and wreak havoc. We must learn to respond to each other instead of reacting; we should think before we speak.

The longer I live, the more I realize the impact of attitude on life. Attitude is more important than facts. It is more important than anything we think or say or do. We cannot change the fact that people will act a certain way. We cannot change the inevitable. The only thing we can do is play on the string we have, and that is our attitude.

We may think that humility is allowing someone to walk all over us. Let us clarify "humility." Jesus brought about the recognition of His humility by demonstrating absolute dependence on the Father. Jesus said, "I do nothing of myself but as my Father hath taught me, I speak these things" (John 8:28). Humility really means that we are willing to say and agree with what our Father has to say about the situation.

The Holy Spirit gives infinite wisdom and instruction. His heart's desire is for relationship with us.

I will give them a heart to know me, that I am the Lord. They will be my people, and I will be their God, for they will return to me with all their heart" (Jeremiah 24:7 NIV).

His love is so *great* for us that He sent the Helper, the Holy Spirit. As we seek His counsel, He will direct us in all things. A married couple gets wisdom from the Holy Spirit when their spirits (hearts) are joined with His. He is the Third Cord, the Cord that permanently bonds husband and wife together.

A PRAYER FOR YOUR MARRIAGE

Dear Lord,
You have given us every tool we need for having a successful marriage. Our commitment to You and our spouse is forever. Thank You that as we are unified by the Third Cord we experience Your power to achieve success in our marriage.

If you are ready to receive the ability to "pray in the Spirit," pray this prayer . . .

Thank You, Father, that I may receive intimacy with You on a deeper level by praying in the Spirit. I am asking today that You allow me that privilege. It is a special prayer language that will not sound of this world. Just as Acts 2:3-4 (NASB) says, "And there appeared to them (on the day of Pentecost) tongues as of fire distributing themselves, and they rested on each one of them. And they were all filled with the Holy Spirit and began to speak with other tongues, as the Spirit was giving them utterance," so do I by faith receive that gift today. Lead me in its operation in my life. In Jesus' name, amen.

In Closing: A Note from the Authors

Henry Wadsworth Longfellow was filled with sorrow at the tragic death of his wife in a fire in 1861. The Civil War broke out that same year, and it seemed this was an additional punishment. Two years later, Longfellow was again saddened to hear that his son had been seriously wounded as a lieutenant in the Army of the Potomac. Sitting down to his desk one Christmas day, he heard the church bells ringing. It was at this time he wrote:

I heard the bells on Christmas day
Their old familiar carols play
And wild and sweet the words repeat
Of peace on earth good will to men.

And in despair I bowed my head
There is no peace on earth I said
For fate is strong and mocks the song
Of peace on earth, good will to men.

Then peeled the bells more loud and deep,
God is not dead, nor doth He sleep
The wrong shall fail, the right prevail
With peace on earth, good will to men.

In knowing the inspiration of this hymn, I trust you will understand it with new-found significance. Despite Longfellow's time of hopelessness, he did not lose heart or hope. Instead, he was able to find hope. Our prayer for you is that by reading this book, you will have a renewed hope in your marriage. We would like to encourage you to invite the Holy Spirit into your marriage every day and watch to see the secrets He will reveal to you. May you discover the wisdom of the Holy Spirit together.

Our final prayer is that you may begin to see your spouse through new eyes and that God will give you beauty for ashes in your marriage relationship.

Our most sincere blessing to you,
Alan and Jamie Wood